RELAX...YOU'RE NOT GOING TO DIE - PART I

More Spiritual Insights for Your Life

DARRYL J PHILIP, COPYRIGHT 2015

3/2/2016

Culmination of spiritual viewpoints from our contemporary messengers of God, our near-death experiencers, our gifted psychic mediums, our courageous scientists and researchers, and ancient spiritual wisdom are revealing God's plan for us.

ISBN: 0995076103
ISBN 13: 9780995076105

RELAX...YOU'RE NOT GOING TO DIE - PART I

I dedicate this book in memory of my wonderful mother:

Cynthia Philip

ACKNOWLEDGEMENTS

I would like to express my deepest thanks and appreciation to God, for all the inspiration and guidance in writing this book. I thank my family and friends for tolerating my time away from them, while writing this book. This book would not be possible without the contemporary messengers of God. Thank you to Neale Donald Walsch for authoring the Conversation with God books (CWG) and the late Helen Schucman and the late Bill Thetford for providing "A Course in Miracles" (ACIM). I would like to thank all of the near-death experiencers that told their stories and documented their spiritual insights: Mr. Dannion Brinkley, Ms. Betty Eadie, Dr. Eben Alexander, Dr. Mary C. Neal and Ms. Anita Moorjani. I'm grateful to the gifted psychics; Mr. Roy Mills for providing his spiritual insights, including the team of gifted psychics that worked with Robert Schwartz in creating his book "Your Soul's Plan": Ms. Deb Debari, Ms. Glenna Dietrich, Ms. Corbie Mitleid and Ms. Staci Wells; Thank you to all the courageous, scientists, doctors and researchers that documented their scientific insights. Dr. Raymond Moody, Dr. Melvin L. Morse,

Dr. Dean Radin, Ms. Lynne McTaggart, Dr. Masaru Emoto, Mr. Lee Strobel, Mr. Robert Schwartz, Dr. Kenneth Ring, Dr. Sharon Cooper, Dr. Gary Schwarz, Dr. Robert Lanza, Dr. Gerald Sittser, Dr. Sam Parnia, the late Elizabeth Claire Prophet, Ms. the late Michael Talbot, Karen Armstrong and Dr. Michael Abrams. This book would not be possible without the permissions, from the publishers to use specific quotes from their published works. I'm truly grateful to the following publishers who permitted me to use the various quotes throughout this book: Hampton Roads Publishing Company (New York, NY), Penguin Putman Inc., (New York, NY), The Foundation for Inner Peace (Mill Valley, CA) Onjinjinkta Publishing (Seattle, WA), Frog Books (Berkeley, CA) Zondervan (Grand Rapids MI), Penguin Random House Publishing (New York, NY), HarperCollins Publishing (New York, NY), HarperCollins Christian Publishing (Grand Rapids, MI) Hay House (Carlsbad, CA), Simon & Schuster Inc. (New York, NY), Summit University Press (Gardiner, MT)

Thank you to Ms. Raeanne Pearce at Tellwell Publishing in Victoria, British Columbia, for assisting me with the first rounds of editing and the great editing team at CreateSpace. Last, but not least, I'd like to thank the early reviewers that volunteered their time and energy to review the initial manuscript and provide feedback: Mr. Lloyd Pollard, Mr. Paget Warner and Ms. Katerina Kojatchenko.

TABLE OF CONTENTS

A COURSE IN MIRACLES REFERENCE

Many of the quotations used in this book came from *A Course in Miracles*, combined volume (ACIM). The use of ACIM quotations were kindly and generously provided by the publisher "Foundation of Inner Peace". This is a brief reference to allow readers to locate the various quotations used in this book.

A Course in Miracles consists of three main books:

1. Text (T)
2. Workbook for Students (W)
3. Manual for Teachers (M)

Each quotation and endnote from ACIM includes a notation. Please follow these examples to locate and refer to these quotation in the ACIM.

T-9.VIII.7:1-6 From the ACIM Text, chapter 9, section VIII, paragraph 7, sentences 1 to 6.

T	- Text
9	- Chapter 9
VIII	- Section VIII
7	- Paragraph no.
1-6	- Sentences 1 to 6

W-P1.62.3:1 From the ACIM Workbook for Students, part 1, lesson 62, paragraph 3, sentence 1.

W	- Workbook for Students
P1	- Part 1
62	- Lesson 62
3	- Paragraph 3
1	- Sentence number 1

M-12.3:2 Manual for Teachers, question 12, paragraph 3, sentence 2

M	- Manual for Teachers
12	- Question 12,
3	- Paragraph 3
2	- Sentence number 2

INTRODUCTION

Have you ever wondered what it is you're doing here? I'm not just talking about your immediate physical location on this earth, but what is it that you're doing here in this lifetime? Why here, and why now? There are a multitude of places in this enormous universe where you could be right now, so why here? Most of us would assume that our parents got together and had a child or some children and we just happen to be one of them. We're currently living out our lives, one day at a time, like other human beings on this earth. Well, you may be surprised to learn that with the new insights gained from our contemporary messengers of God, our near-death experiencers, our gifted psychics, our courageous scientists, and ancient spiritual wisdom, we are finally beginning to piece together a better understanding of God and life. Despite what you might think or believe, our lives are not just some inconsequential, pointless event playing out in this apparently chaotic world. Our lives are much more significant than that and we are much more powerful and magnificent beings than we are led to believe. This lifetime is not just an exercise in meaningless suffering. I would never presume to know God's entire plan for you and me, but a culmination of evidence is allowing us to at least get a glimpse of God's plan.

We know today that God loves unconditionally. God's love and compassion for us is unwavering and unlimited! You, me, and all of us are godly and immortal beings who will never die! Life and death are all part of the same unending journey taking us to spiritual mastery. Irrespective of the trials, setbacks, and circumstances that we encounter in life, our lives are more perfect than we can even imagine. I invite you to join me on this excursion of self-discovery to confront and address some of our most perplexing questions about God and life.

Chapter 1

A SEARCH FOR TRUTH BEGINS

*"To remember is merely to restore to your
mind what is already there. You do not make
what you remember, you merely accept again
what is already there, but was rejected."*

GOD-THROUGH-HELEN SCHUCMAN, (ACIM, T-10.II.3:1,2)

This journey began because I was a curious kid with questions.
I was always asking myself questions, such as: "What am I doing here?" For me, it was perfectly reasonable to assume that I
could be any number of places in the universe. Why here and
why now? My parents had immigrated from the Caribbean country of Trinidad and Tobago to attend the University of British
Columbia. Subsequently, both my sister and I were born in
Vancouver, Canada. Initially, my parents had come to Canada
holding tightly to their faith and Catholic/Christian beliefs.
Growing up in a Christian family, my older sister Mel and I

would regularly attend Sunday school while our parents attended church, each and every Sunday. I would listen attentively to the Sunday school teachers and church pastor as they quoted holy scripture from the Bible and explained to us the deeper meaning of God and Life. In the Christian church, we were taught several religious doctrines:

* God is an all-powerful, male figure living in Heaven.
* God still requires and needs certain things from us.
* Belief and adherence to Christianity is the one and only true path to God.
* You and I are separate from God.
* We are all inherent sinners who were born in sin and remain imperfect in the eyes of God.
* God loves us all very much, but under certain conditions God could become displeased.
* God's displeasure could turn into anger and God's anger would manifest in wrath and retribution.
* Finally, if you should fail to obey God's laws, then God would send you to Hell - a place with endless torment and unspeakable suffering.

These are just some of the main doctrines and dogmas taught from the pulpits, not only from the Christian Church, but also from many of the world's major religions. It's true that not all religions teach these beliefs, but I'm referring to our major religions - those religions that claim that theirs is the only one true path to God. These are the religions that separate their followers from the other followers of God. These are the types of religions that teach about a wrathful and vengeful male God who could and would punish you with eternal damnation.

As I grew into my teens, I always had a genuine curiosity about God and life. Talking with members of the Church and poring over holy scripture was not enough to satisfy my curiosity. In some cases, church members would not even discuss my questions, and would instead simply refer me back to the Bible to find the answers I sought.

In my experience, what I find most confusing about studying the Bible is the constant contradictions between biblical verses. In one verse you have God's forgiveness, while in the next verse you're the victim of God's wrath. One verse tells you to love thy neighbor, and the next verse tells you to stone thy neighbor to death at the town gates! It was all very confusing.

A main doctrine of Christianity tells followers that Christianity is the only true path to God, but what of the many indigenous people, born into tribes, in the very remote regions of the earth? How are they supposed to hear "the word of God", and what would happen to them if they should never hear the word of God? When I posed this question to one Christian pastor, he said to me, "I'm afraid that those poor souls are all lost." By "lost", he meant that they would never see heaven nor be with God because they had not received any of the Christian teachings. This implied that a loving and caring God would have some people born in a time, place, and circumstance where it would be extremely difficult to receive any religious teachings, yet when they fail to receive the word of God, they are punished with separation from God and eternal damnation? This didn't make any sense to me. Religion could never provide the reason for the inherent inequalities that we see in life. For example, some of us are born with physical and emotional challenges or economic disadvantage. I had faith that

God was there, but for me, religion could not provide satisfactory answers - if religion could even answer the questions at all.

Quite unintentionally, I began to do my own research to try and make some sense of my life purpose and my relationship to God. It was the early eighties and I started to look at what was considered at the time unconventional reference materials. A young medical doctor by the name of Raymond A. Moody Jr. had just published a book called *Life after Life*. Dr. Moody was really the first to blaze a trail into the unchartered territory of what's become commonly known as the "near-death experience"[1] or NDE. As medical resuscitation techniques improved, more and more people who were presumed dead were brought back to life with intriguing stories of being outside their bodies, travelling through tunnels, conversing with a being of light, and witnessing a life review. Back in the eighties, I was an avid patron of "The Learning Annex", a continuing education program for adults. The Learning Annex offered a variety of short evening and weekend courses - everything from Thai cooking and computer courses to sailing and golf lessons. Another category was New Age Spirituality. It was here that I went to listen to near-death experiencers such as Dannion Brinkley and Betty Eadie.

I'm not a near-death experiencer (NDEcr), nor am I a gifted psychic or medium. I can't even say that I'm a highly educated, well-credentialed scientist exploring the new frontiers of human consciousness. However, we all have an inner voice which guides us in our life journey, but it also tells us if what we're listening to is true or false. After carefully reading Moody's book and listening firsthand to the eye witness accounts of the near-death experience, my inner voice told me that the near-death experience was a true human experience. Today, with the growing mountain of medical documentation and plethora of accounts by near-death experiencers, even mainstream science is beginning to accept the fact that our consciousness survives death. It was my hope that by looking at the NDE, I could gain a broader perspective and a deeper understanding of my life purpose and my relationship with God.

As I looked at more accounts of the NDE, I didn't second guess the survival of the spirit; after all, our religions and our great spiritual teachers have been telling us this for thousands and thousands of years. However, I did have lingering questions about the afterlife and whether or not a soul could be sentenced to an eternity in Hell.

By the late sixties, our family had moved from Vancouver BC to Toronto, Ontario where my parents had found employment. My father started as a social worker while my mother worked as a dietitian at the Wellesley Hospital in downtown Toronto. By the mid-seventies Dad was a different man. He had long stopped going to church and his work-life had become too busy for God, religion, and even family. He was caught up in his new teaching career and had begun to dabble in the real estate market, but his biggest transformation was in his faith. He was now a self-professed atheist living his life with no belief in God or religion. At some point in the mid-seventies, Mom and Dad separated and eventually divorced.

Moving forward to the early eighties, both my parents had remarried. Mom had reconnected with a long lost love in Trinidad and was preparing to return there to live and retire. They say that there's a silver lining behind every dark cloud. Well, in this case, it was my new stepmom Nancy and a beautiful, new little sister named Heather from Dad's second marriage. While attending university, I lived with Dad, Nancy, and Heather. Life wasn't always perfect, but we all got along as mature adults and I had the opportunity to get to know and love Nancy and Heather - the newest member of the family.

By the late eighties Dad's health was beginning to give him problems. He had lived with a minor heart condition for decades and his pack-a-day cigarette smoking was not helping. Earlier in his life doctors had recommended heart surgery, but with Dad always fearful and distrustful of doctors and hospitals, he refused to have the surgery done. When I was younger, I would pray fervently to God to protect and watch over my Dad. I was always anxious that some tragic event would befall him, like having a heart-attack shoveling the snow or getting into a very serious car accident. One hot summer day in August, Dad went out to run some errands and suffered a serious stroke.

The stroke affected Dad's speech, memory, and thought patterns. He experienced difficulty remembering things like names, places, and events. The stroke prevented him from going back to teaching, and all of these ailments in his life put a strain on his marriage to Nancy. By the early nineties Dad was divorced again and out of work. He came to live with me and my then fiancée - Carol. It was during this time I could clearly see that in addition to his health problems, he was also suffering from some dementia. Despite the condition of his health and mind, Dad never accepted the fact that he was ill. Instead, he insisted on being independent - going out and running various errands of great importance. We would come home from work on Friday evening only to receive a message from the local transit authority office telling us that Dad was downtown at some subway station confused and disoriented.

Over time the dementia became worse. We worried about my Dad using the stove, taking his medication regularly, and leaving the house during the day while we were away at work. With reluctance, we had no choice but to find a nursing home where he could be cared for twenty-four seven. Initially, Dad was put on a waiting list until a spot opened up. We eventually found a small place about twenty minutes from our home. Some three months after being admitted to the nursing home, Dad succumbed to congestive heart failure - he was sixty-nine.

Even though Dad had been sick for some time, I was still shocked and saddened by his death. The truth is we were never really that close, not only because we had very different interests but also because we hadn't spent a lot of time together. There's nothing to be gained by going into the details here - we all have our shortcomings. Given his upbringing and model of the world, I think he tried to be the best father that he could be. As a result of his life, I now know how I can be a better father in my own family. Later in the summer of that same year, Carol and I got married.

Given Dad's chaotic life and his self-proclaimed atheism, I wasn't too sure where Dad's spirit was or if he was at peace. I wasn't sure what to think, but around three or four weeks after Dad's passing, one of the most remarkable and astonishing things in my life happened. The event would drastically change my outlook of God and life forever. In fact, this event would provide the impetus in my ongoing search for truth and lay the foundations for writing this book: I saw my father in a dream! In this dream, I found myself back in our old house where I grew up in Scarborough, Ontario. In the dream, my Dad came through the door, just like he was coming home from work. He was wearing his hat with a grey suit and a familiar beige trench coat. As he came through the door, he began to remove his hat and coat, as if to put them away in the closet. He looked like he was a little younger. He looked healthy and he no longer had his portable oxygen tank. This was a complete surprise. Incredulously, I exclaimed, "Dad!?" and he very casually answered back, "I'm alright" - that was it! I awoke almost immediately and said to my new wife Carol, "I just saw Dad." Instantly, two thoughts came into my head. The first thought was I think that Dad made it to heaven. The second thought was that this God is truly a loving and forgiving God.

To some this dream will sound strange or untrue, and I can understand that. If the experience hadn't happened to me, given what I know about my father's life I wouldn't believe it either. But more than a decade after I had this dream, I still remember it clearly. One of my heroes, the Archbishop Desmond Tutu was quoted as saying *We may be surprised at the people we find in heaven. God has a soft spot for sinners. His standards are quite low.*[2]

I've since learned that this type of dream is called a "lucid dream". Dreaming of deceased loved ones is really a lot more common than we know. The writing team of Bill and Judy Guggenheim have researched and compiled a study of these events and have called them "after death communications" or ADCs. Bill and Judy claim that their ADC project took seven years to fulfill its purpose. During this time they collected more than 3,300 firsthand accounts of after-death communications by interviewing

2,000 people who live in all fifty American states and the ten Canadian provinces. These people are from all walks of life and represent diverse social, educational, occupational, and economic backgrounds. They range in age from an eight-year-old boy to a ninety-two-year-old widower.[3] Bill and Judy have compiled the stories of these people, events, and experiences in their wonderful book entitled *Hello from Heaven! A new field of research - After-Death-Communication Confirms that Life and Love are Eternal.*

The Guggenheims point out that psychologists, psychiatrists, bereavement counselors, members of the clergy, and others have historically dismissed these experiences as hallucinations, delusions, or fantasies. The traditional viewpoint has been that ADCs are the result of wish fulfillment, imagination, magical thinking, or memories caused by grief. In fact, they have usually been called "grief-induced hallucinations".[4]

I stumbled upon another instance of an ADC, quite by accident, while researching this book. I was in the kitchen one Saturday morning having a casual conversation with Grannie. My wife's grandmother, who we affectionately call "Grannie", has been living with us for the past ten years. I'll refer to her here as "Violet". Aside from her regular, weekly activities Violet also enjoys watching a little television, and one of those shows that she enjoys is a fishing reality show. One morning over breakfast I asked Violet if she had ever gone fishing in her childhood. She had been born and raised in Guyana and had come to Canada in her adult years. She couldn't recall ever going fishing as a child, but this discussion prompted memories of a younger sister named Alice who had passed away when Violet was only fourteen years old.

In Guyana at that time, there were numerous irrigation canals built to support Guyana's government-sponsored agricultural program. Violet explained that one of their neighbors had a small boat that he kept docked in one of the canals. However, this neighbor did not have a paddle for the boat and so he would sometimes call on Violet's family to borrow a paddle. On this day, Violet's mother asked thirteen-year-old Alice to carry the paddle and put it into the neighbor's boat. Alice was given specific instructions to put the paddle into the boat and return home promptly. On the way to the boat, Alice met up with a friend and together they went to deliver the paddle. However, once they arrived, they decided to go into the boat and start playing around. Suddenly, a gust of wind blew the small boat away from the shore and out into the canal. Alice, who was unfamiliar with boats and unable to swim, went into a panic and jumped off the boat into the deep water of the canal in a frenzied effort to get back to the shore. The young girl quickly drowned in the deep waters of the canal. They later learned that a passerby had seen Alice jump from the boat, but was too far away to rescue her.

The family was unware of the tragic accident and only realized that something was amiss because they heard the commotion outside and noticed people in the village running up the road towards the canal. Violet, who was only fourteen at the time, left the house to find out what all the fuss was about. As she approached the canal a villager came running up to her and said, "Your sister…Your sister!" That is how she found out about Alice's fatal accident.

Over the next few weeks, the grief that the family felt was almost unbearable, but for Violet, losing her younger sister was absolutely devastating. She found it terribly difficult to think of anything else. She all but stopped eating and subsequently developed a serious gastro condition. Around this time, she recalls having had a dream. In this dream, she saw her sister Alice looking healthy and happy. Alice said to her in a very concerned and serious tone, "What has happened to you? Look at what you are doing to yourself! Come...follow me, I have to show you something." She followed Alice down to a river bank. There, Alice picked some leaves from a small guava tree and clenched the leaves in her hand. She then plunged her clenched hand into the river water and said to Violet, "Open your mouth." As Violet opened her mouth, Alice squeezed the water from the wet leaves into Violet's mouth.

With that, Violet awoke from her dream and told her mother that she had seen Alice. She conveyed to her mother what had transpired in the dream and her mother, recognizing the significance of the event, told Violet to go out right away and gather some guava leaves to make a tea. Violet went out and collected some guava leaves to make tea. Once she drank the homemade tea, her stomach ailments quickly subsided and shortly after completely disappeared.

This is an ADC that Grannie described to me, though she was completely unaware that I had any prior interest in ADC. What is more fascinating to me is that Grannie was ninety-two years old at the time and she still remembered this dream clearly!

The Guggenheims point out that ADCs are very common in other parts of the world where they are socially accepted as real communications from deceased loved ones. The people who have these experiences are able to share them freely and joyously with others, and everyone gains from discussing these events openly.

Hopefully after-death communication will one day gain the same degree of public awareness and acceptance in our own culture.[5]

After Dad's ADC, I had no doubts that his spirit continues to live on in a much better place. I stopped to contemplate what else I may not know about God and life.

Chapter 2

AN OPENNESS TO LEARNING

*"It was only when you stopped fearing Me that you could
create any kind of meaningful relationship with Me.
If I could give you any gift, any special grace, that
would allow you to find Me, it would be fearlessness.
Blessed are the fearless, for they shall know God."*

God-through-Neale Donald Walsh,
Conversations with God Book 3

One life lesson that I've come across is the advantage of keeping an open mind and a willingness to learn. Just when you think you have it all figured out, just when you believe that you know it all, there is always more to know. This applies whether you're baking cookies, tending a garden, performing a delicate surgery, or building a rocket ship. As a matter of fact, it is this openness to learning that propels technology, psychology, science, business, and even nutrition. In all these areas, we have shown an openness to learning and acceptance of new ideas and innovation. Unfortunately, this has not been the case when it comes to God. To learn about God we look to our religions, but the truth is that our religions have not explored a significant, new idea about God in thousands of years. We haven't had an extension of our theologies in a hundred generations. The very thought of introducing a new idea is a violation of strongly held religious doctrine.[6]

Today, we have much greater insights into God and life coming from the millions of NDErs, our gifted mediums and psychics, God's own contemporary messengers, after-death communications, and yes, even the progressive and courageous doctors and scientists in our medical and scientific community are contributing to a new understanding about God and life. I would stress here that this is a new understanding and not necessarily new information. All of our great spiritual teachers - The Buddha, Joseph Smith, Mohammed, Moses, Jesus, and others - have brought this information to us before, but now we're finally beginning to validate it and see its truth.

Before we enter too far into this discussion, I want to say something right up front. I want to be very clear that I have a great respect for all organized religions. It is not my intention to promote any one religion over another or any one spiritual teacher over another. While it's true that I have had a Christian upbringing, this is not about promoting Christianity. This is more about revealing some broad spiritual insights that apply to all of us across the boundaries of religion, culture, race, gender, sexual orientation, social class, and age.

Throughout human history, most of us believe that God has spoken to human beings through other human beings at one time or another. We just don't believe that it still happens today. We believe that all of the information about God was given two thousand years ago. Everything there is to know about God is already known. Everything there is to say about God has already been said. There can be no new spiritual revelations about God today, or can there?[7] On the contrary, we have a plentiful supply of evidence that God is still talking to human beings and has never stopped talking to human beings even today.

> *"That means you must be fearless enough to drop what you think you know about God.*
> *You must be fearless enough to step away from what others have told you about God.*
> *You must be so fearless that you can dare to enter into your own experience of God."*[8]

> *God-through-Neale Donald Walsch.*

I find my spiritual inspiration through God, meditation, people, and books. In addition to God's inspiration and the documented eye witness accounts of the NDE, two of my most inspirational sources have been the *Conversations with God* books and *A Course in Miracles*. These books inspire me because they align with my own intuitive inner truth and knowing; they are spiritually uplifting and reflect the thoughts and words of a God of unconditional love and compassion. I sincerely believe that these writers are our contemporary messengers of God. Last but not least, our medical and scientific communities are now confirming much of what is written inside of their pages.

Neale Donald Walsch is the author of *Conversations with God* Books One, Two, and Three. His is an interesting story about how he came to have a conversation with God. It occurs in the spring of 1992, when Neale has just turned fifty and his life has hit an extremely low point. He's struggling in his personal relationships, he's having health problems, and it is not the best of times for his career. One night, as these worries and negative thoughts are circling around in his head, he's unable to sleep and so he reaches for what he calls his "trusty legal writing pad". He has decided to express his anger and resentment by writing an angry letter to God. Neale explains:

> *"This time, rather than another letter to another person I imagined to be victimizing me, I thought I'd go straight to the source; straight to the greatest victimizer of them all. I decided to write a letter to God. It was a spiteful, passionate letter, full of confusions, contortions, and condemnations. And a pile of angry questions. Why wasn't my life working? What would it take to get it to work? Why could I not find happiness in relationships? Was the experience of adequate money going to elude me forever? Finally - and most emphatically - What had I done to deserve a life of such continuing struggle?"[9]*

Much to Neale's surprise, he begins to hear an inner voice in his head - a response from God. The *Conversations with God* books provides a detailed account of this conversation between Neale and God. I sincerely believe that this is God talking to all of us through Neale. When I quote passages from this book, I'll just call it "God-through-Neale".

The second source is *A Course in Miracles* authored by the late Dr. Helen Schucman and the late Dr. Bill Thetford back in 1965. At the time both Helen and Bill were career-oriented psychologists working closely together at the Columbia-Presbyterian Medical Center where they were attempting to develop and strengthen the Center's Psychology Department. While they had similar professional interests and goals for the department, their personalities clashed and they had frequent disagreements. In the Spring of 1965 Bill decided to end their constant bickering and competitive aggression towards each other which extended to their attitudes and relationships and pervaded the department. He concluded that "there must be another way of living - in harmony rather than discord" - and he was determined to find it. It was as if Helen had waited all her life for this particular moment, which triggered a series of internal experiences for her that included heighted dream imagery, psychic episodes, visions, and an experience of an inner voice. The experience also became increasingly religious, with the figure of Jesus appearing more and more frequently to her in both visual and auditory expressions. This period of preparation culminated on the evening of October 21, 1965 when the now familiar voice of Jesus said to Helen: "This is a course in miracles, please take notes." Troubled, she called Bill immediately, and he reassured her that she was not going mad. He suggested she write down what was being dictated to her, and that he would look at it with her early the following morning at the office. Helen did just that, which is how the scribing of *A Course in Miracles* began[10]. The whole process would take seven years. As Helen later described the experience:

> *"I was still very surprised when I wrote, 'This is a course in Miracles'. That was my introduction to the Voice.*

The voice made no sound, but seemed to be giving me a kind of rapid, inner dictation, which I took down in a shorthand note-book. The writing was never automatic. It could be interrupted at any time and later picked up again. It made me very uncomfortable, but it never seriously occurred to me to stop. It seemed to be a special assignment I had somehow, somewhere agreed to complete."[11]

When I quote passages from this source, I'll just call it "God-through-Helen".

INSIGHTS FROM NDE

Another great source of spiritual insight and inspiration has come from the eye witness accounts and the documented research of the near-death experiencers (NDEers). Due to the sheer volume, the long history, and the staggering amount of evidence on this subject, we can't really have a serious discussion about human spirituality without addressing the NDE. This human experience is occurring every day in our hospitals across the country. If you're unfamiliar with the NDE experience, it begins like this:

1. Due to some severe physical bodily trauma or illness your spirit separates from the body and you find yourself outside your body, light and more alive than ever. You find yourself floating or hovering over your body, witnessing the entire scene around you, feeling an emotional detachment from the events unfolding.

2. There is a heightened awareness and an altered perspective of time and space. You experience a peacefulness and calm

that you have not known before - free of pain, physical ailments, and worry.

3. You are drawn into a tunnel.

4. You come through the tunnel into a wondrous space of unspeakable beauty and light, where you are greeted or recognized by deceased loved ones and/or a being of light.

5. Eventually, you may find yourself in the presence of a being of light that emanates a feeling of unconditional love, compassion, and acceptance.

6. In a great many cases, this being of light introduces you to a thorough panoramic review of your life, showing you the good and the bad, not only from your point of view, but also from the point of view of the other person or persons affected by your choices, decisions, and actions.

7. Due to unfinished work in your life, you are reluctantly returned to your body.

8. The experience transforms you into a more spiritual and altruistic human being, no longer afraid of death and with a completely revised, positive, vision of God and life.

Of the millions of NDE cases, not everyone has this exact experience - of course there are some variations. For example, some NDErs recall leaving their body and witnessing the resuscitation efforts of the medical staff but never going on to see deceased loved ones or have a life review. However, looking at the thousands of documented cases, what I describe above is more or less the core pattern of the near-death experience.

Moody was a true researcher, blazing a trail for a new generation of researchers: well-educated, well-credentialed medical doctors and psychologists who provided their own investigation and research into the NDE. Dr. Sam Parnia, M.D., Ph.D., is one such medical doctor pursuing his own NDE research. In his book *What Happens When We Die*, Parnia provides this descriptive account of a man who narrowly escaped drowning:

> "Though the senses were...deadened, not so the mind; its activity seemed to be invigorated in a ratio which defies all descriptions, for thought rose about thought in rapid succession. The event just occurred ... the awkwardness producing it...the bustle it must have occasioned...the effect on my most affectionate father...the moment in which it would be disclosed to the family, and a thousand other circumstances minutely associated with home were the first reflections. Then they took a wider range, our last cruise...a former voyage and shipwreck, my school and boyish pursuits and adventures. Thus traveling backwards, every past incident of my life seemed to glance across my recollection in retrograde succession; not however in mere outline, as here stated, but the picture filled up with every minute and collateral feature. In short, the whole period of my existence seemed to be placed before me in a kind of panoramic review, and each part of it seemed to be accompanied by a consciousness of right or wrong, or by some reflection on its cause or consequences; indeed many trifling events which had been forgotten then crowded into my imagination, and with the character of recent familiarity."

Anyone familiar with the NDE will immediately see the tell-tale descriptions from this event - there's nothing new here. Except this is an historical NDE, uncovered in Parnia's research. It is a firsthand account, found in a local newspaper, described by an admiral in the British Navy who almost drowned in Portsmouth Harbour, back in 1795.[12]

SKEPTICISM IS GOOD

With more and more evidence surrounding the NDE, I think that many people are gradually beginning to accept the truth that our consciousness or spirit or essence, whatever you'd like to call it, survives death. Yet despite the mounting evidence, there are still many who remain skeptical and unsure of the NDE. There's nothing wrong with that. It's our God-given right to stand by our beliefs.

Just to re-cap, the skeptics point out that the NDE is nothing more than a brain-based hallucination. That is to say that the experience is based on some kind of a physical, biological reaction in the brain. Skeptics point to several reasons behind the NDE, such as the side effects from medicines or drugs or a lack of oxygen in the blood (a condition known as hypoxia). There is even the theory that the NDE is the last reflex reaction from a dying brain, but all of these theories attach the NDE to nothing more than a function of the physical brain, like walking or lifting your hand to scratch your nose.[13]

Alright, fair enough, but this is what the evidence is showing us today and this why I'm a believer in NDEs. First of all, when you're clinically dead, you should not be having a very clear, visually captivating experience. Dr. Jeffrey Long, a radiation oncologist who has conducted a decade's worth of research on the NDE, makes a compelling case for this in his book, *Evidence of the After Life: The Science of the Near-Death Experience*. Long's reasoning is this: "Speaking both medically and logically, it is not possible to have a highly lucid experience while unconscious or clinically dead. After all, being clinically dead means no longer having the perceptions or senses of a living person."[14]

There is no shortage of eye witness accounts that give very convincing testimony that, even with the absence of vital signs, these NDErs still possessed a good sense of their surroundings and heightened abilities to perceive.

HEIGHTENED PSYCHIC ABILITY

Betty J. Eadie speaks about her NDE and the enhanced psychic abilities in her book *Embraced By The Light*. On November 18, 1973 Betty had entered the hospital to undergo a partial hyster-ectomy.[15] During the procedure doctors scramble to control the bleeding and that night, after the surgery, she begins bleeding out badly again. Later, her doctor would tell her that they almost lost her. During Betty's NDE, the very thought of home takes her there and she reflects about her ability to see into the futures of all her children.

"My trip home was a blur. I began moving at tremendous speed, now that I realized I could, and I was only vaguely aware of trees rushing below me. I made no decisions, gave myself no directions - just the thought of home and I knew I was going there. Within a moment I was at my house and found myself entering the living room. I saw my husband sitting in his favorite armchair reading the newspaper. I saw my children running up and down the stairs and knew that they were supposed to be getting ready for bed. Two of them were in a pillow fight - actually normal bedtime procedure for our children. I had no desire to communicate with them, but I was concerned about their lives without me. As I watched them individu-ally, a preview of sorts ran through my mind about them, enabling me to see ahead into each of their lives. I came to know that each of

my children was on earth for their own experiences, that although I had thought of them as "mine," I had been mistaken. They were individual spirits, like myself, with an intelligence that was developed before their lives on earth. Each one had their own free will to live their life as they chose."[16]

This heightened perception is another reason why I can't accept the NDE as merely a brain-based hallucination.

NEAR-DEATH EXPERIENCES THAT CLEARLY DO NOT INVOLVE THE BRAIN

Two highly trained psychologists and very well credentialed PhDs, Kenneth Ring and Sharon Cooper, are the authors of *MindSight: Near-Death and Out-of-Body Experiences in the Blind.* In this book the authors describe an unusual study they conducted to determine if NDEs were connected to the physical brain. Unlike other researchers who have typically conducted their research on subjects with no visual impairment, Ring and Cooper decided to study the NDE in the blind. In their study they had fourteen respondents who were blind from birth.[17]

For you and I to have cognitive vision, it means that every part of our optical system must be functioning: not just the retina and neighboring neurons in our eyes, but also the occipital lobe of the brain in the back of our heads[18]. It follows that if the NDE are really just brain-based and the hallucinations of physiologically impaired brains, then the blind should not have any visuals during an NDE. After this scientific study of NDE in the blind, Ring and Cooper came to this conclusion:

"Our findings here were unequivocal in the affirmative. There is no question that NDEs in the blind do occur and furthermore, that they take the same general form and are comprised of the very same elements that define the NDEs of sighted individuals. Moreover, this generalization appears to hold across all three categories of blindness that were represented in this study: those blind from birth, the adventitiously blind and the severely visually impaired."

"The second issue, and the one that was the driving force of this study, was of course whether the blind claim to have visual impressions during the NDEs or OBEs (out-of-body experiences). On this point, too, our data were conclusive. Overall 80% of our respondents reported these claims, most of them in the language of unhesitating declaration, even when they may have been surprised, or even stunned, by the unexpected discovery that they could in fact see. Like sighted experiencers, our blind respondents described to us both perceptions of this world as well as otherworldly scenes, often in fulsome, fine-grained detail, and sometimes with a sense of extremely sharp, even subjectively perfect, acuity."[19]

Ring's and Cooper's detailed study of NDEs in the blind and visually impaired provide even more evidence against the idea that NDEs are only brain based.

THE PERSONAL TRANSFORMATION

Personal transformation has to do with the "after effects" of the NDE. Research into the NDE has revealed that NDErs typically experience a dramatic, personal transformation after they've had the experience. These lasting personal transformations are positive and profoundly change the individual into a more loving, caring, altruistic, and spiritual human being. In addition, these individuals no longer carry any fear of death or dying because they are certain of their continued existence. They've had the experience and so there are no doubts. On the contrary, they see a greater purpose for their lives and are inspired to live life to its fullest. Career criminals are transformed into counsellors who help troubled youth, workaholics become more loving and caring towards their families, and individuals who were previously impatient and/or short-tempered become more easy-going and tolerant. The NDEr is also less concerned with material items and the pursuit of worldly possessions after having the experience. In several cases, the NDE is credited with increasing the individual's intuition and perception, as in the case of Dannion Brinkley. Back on September 17th, 1975, Dannion had a near-death experience when he was struck by lightning. He documented his experience in his book *At Peace in the Light*. I feel a special connection with Dannion because while he was on the speaking circuit, he came to Toronto. I went to hear him speak and had the opportunity to meet him in person. In his early days of recovery, when he was just strong enough to leave the hospital and take short trips out of the house, he noticed his new enhanced abilities: *"When I was awake, I was picking up thoughts and images from the minds of people I didn't even know. I could look out the window of my house and pick up the thoughts of people walking down the street."*[20]

In his book *Closer to the Light* Dr. Melvin L. Morse, MD studied the NDE in children, and also noticed this transforming effect of the experience. Morse recalls the claims from one of his former patients: *"One woman, for instance, told me that her NDE gave her the 'power to read minds.' By that, she didn't mean that she could read them like a book. 'I have just become very intuitive and can understand how others think. This has helped me in my job as a nurse.'*[21]

Numerous incidents like these prompted Morse to write:

"The effects that such events have on the lives (and deaths) of those who have them are 'proof enough' for me. My research team has documented the transformative power of the NDEs in the people who have them. These transformations are healthy ones, emphasizing a job and devotion to life. One person told me that her experience taught her that 'grief is growth.' Another person learned that everything in this world is interconnected and that whatever problems one faces, there is a reason for that problem. The knowledge that a loving bright light awaits us all at the point of death seems to generate an excitement and dedication to living life to its fullest before joining the light."[22]

Dr. Robert Lanza, MD, is one of the most respected scientists in the world—a U.S. News & World Report cover story called him a "genius" and a "renegade thinker" and likened him to Einstein. He is currently chief scientific officer at Advanced Cell Technology and an adjunct professor at Wake University School of Medicine.[23] In his book *Biocentrism, How Life and Consciousness are the Keys to Understanding the True Nature of the Universe*, Lanza eloquently explains that medical science has long since known that we are beings with an electrical charge. That's to say, that while we are alive, we carry an electrical charge of approximately 100 watts – just like a light bulb. Lanza gives us a purely scientific explanation, based on the nature of energy, for why he is certain that human consciousness continues to exist even after death. Lanza states:

> *"We even emit the same heat as a bulb, too, which is why a car rapidly gets warmer, even during a cold night, especially when a driver is accompanied by a passenger or two. Now the truly skeptical might argue that this internal energy merely "goes away" at death and vanishes. But one of the surest axioms of science is that energy can never die, ever. Energy is known with scientific certainty to be deathless; it can neither be created nor destroyed. Similarly, the essence of who you are, which is energy, can neither diminish nor "go away"---there simply isn't any "away" in which to go. We inhabit a closed system."[24]*

After researching several eye witness accounts of the NDE, I cannot dismiss the NDE as simply a brain-based hallucination for three reasons. First, current medical science tells us that we are not supposed to have a lucid, memorable experience of light when we are clinically dead. Second, NDE involves a very heightened ability to perceive events that defy time and space. Finally, you have the profound and positive transformation of the individuals that have the NDE. I noticed this when I listened to Betty Eadie and Dannion Brinkley speak of their personal experience. I'm in complete agreement with Moody when he writes: *"There is something very persuasive about seeing a person describe his experience which cannot easily be conveyed in writing. Their near-death experiences were very real events to these people, and through my association with them the experiences have become real events to me."[25]*

In the four chapters to follow, I'd like to look at the firsthand eye witness accounts of the NDE from four different and very reliable people. I believe that these four NDEs serve to provide us with a broader, deeper perspective of God and life.

Chapter 3

YOU ARE MORE THAN JUST A BODY - THE NDE OF DRS. MARY C. NEAL, MD

*"The Message here is that you are not your body at
all. You are the essence of that which breathed life
into your body. This is the key. This is the core."*

GOD-THROUGH-NEALE, *THE NEW REVELATIONS:
A CONVERSATION WITH GOD*

For someone to have a real NDE experience is nothing short of extraordinary. They remind me of travelers who have returned from the fabled "promised land". I think that the real treasures, not just for the NDEr but for all of us, are the invaluable spiritual insights that they have brought back from the experience. The travelers have had the extremely rare opportunity to step outside from this ongoing, physical, journey of life and really see it for what it is. In this chapter, we will look at some specific examples of an NDE and get a firsthand, eye witness account from the near-death experiencer.

In the first case, we look at the NDE of Mary C. Neal, MD, an orthopedic surgeon, loving wife, and mother who documents her experience in her book *To Heaven and Back, A Doctor's Extraordinary Account of her Death, Angels, and Life Again.* In addition to Mary's many talents, she is also an avid kayaker. On January 14th, 1999, while on vacation with her husband and friends in South America, Mary goes on a kayaking trip. The beginning of her journey takes place on a river in the remote regions of Chile. While kayaking over a steep waterfall, the bow of her kayak plunges down into the large rocks at the bottom of the falls and becomes lodged in rocks. The kayak is stuck beneath the raging waterfall and Mary is helplessly pinned inside of the kayak, completely inundated by the waterfall rushing over her. Her last recollection is being pulled from her kayak by the raging river current and the sensation of being pushed along the river bottom where she eventually drowns, dies, and goes to heaven. After a brief stay, she returns to her body with two shattered legs and severe pulmonary problems. She is then hospitalized for more than a month, wheelchair-bound for even longer, and does not return to her orthopedic surgery practice for more than six months.[26] Mary describes the very moment she is separated from her body:

> "At the moment my body was released and began to tumble, I felt a 'pop'. It felt as if I had finally shaken off my heavy outer layer, freeing my soul. I rose up and out of the river, and when my soul broke through the surface of the water, I encountered a group of fifteen to twenty souls (human spirits sent by God), who greeted me with the most overwhelming joy I have ever experienced and

could ever imagine. There was joy at an unadulterated core level. They were sort of like a large welcoming committee or a great cloud of witnesses as described in Hebrews 12:1 (ESV)." [27]

In Mary's NDE, she is joyously met by a group of souls: family and friends that she had known in life. As is the case with so many NDErs, she cannot begin to describe the beauty and light of the spiritual realm. When NDErs speak about their experience, words are never enough to describe the spiritual realm, which is God's world and our true home. As Mary attempts to describe the spiritual world, she makes it clear that there is absolutely no comparison to the love of God:

"Don't get me wrong ... I've have been very blessed in my life and have experienced great joy and love here on earth. I love my husband and I love each of my children with great intensity, and that love is reciprocated. It's just that God's world is exponentially more colorful and intense. It was as though I was experiencing an explosion of love and joy in their absolute unadulterated essence." [28]

Today, more and more of us are becoming aware of the power of prayer. Science is also confirming this, but we will discuss more about that later. As Mary is taking great pleasure in this joyous reunion with her dearly departed family and friends, she has all but forgotten her earthly life and the frantic scene taking place down on the banks of the river. By this time, her close friends and kayaking companions have retrieved her body from the river and are now trying desperately to revive her. However, in the spiritual realm, she is totally absorbed in the bliss and ecstasy and is quite prepared to begin the journey to, as Mary puts it, her "eternal home". Mary is still able to look back at the chaotic scene down on the river bank and can actually feel the desperate panic and fear of her friends as they make a frantic attempt to resuscitate her. Even though she feels no emotional attachment to her body and the scene now taking place on the river bank, the prayers and cries for her return affect her. In other words, the constant prayer and beseeching from her companions impede her ability to move on in the spiritual realm. This effect is so strong that it almost becomes annoying to her:

> "There was one notable obstacle to my reunion: Tom Long and his boys kept beckoning to me. Each time they begged me to come back and take a breath, I felt compelled to return to my body and take another breath before returning to my journey. This became tiresome, and I grew quite irritated with their repeated calling. I knew they didn't understand what was happening, but I was annoyed that they wouldn't let me go. I liken it to the irritation that a parent feels when their young child keeps asking for more things before going to bed: a story, a glass of water, the light on, the light off, the covers arranged, another kiss, and so on."[29]

This is an interesting insight because many of us are skeptical about our prayers being heard or greatly underestimate the power of prayer. In another case from *Hello From Heaven*, in an after death communication the deceased loved one returns in a dream to address the chronic, long standing grief of a family member. In this instance the deceased loved one takes a stance of tough love and says to the grieving family member "you have to stop wishing me back" and let go because it is holding back their progression on the other side.[30] Mary's NDE demonstrates that our prayers and our thoughts are felt by our loved ones on the other side.

Eventually, Mary must face the disappointment that she cannot stay in this heavenly realm because her work on earth is not yet finished - it is not yet her time. As is so common in the NDE, she reluctantly returns to her body to carry on with her work and she brings to us her fascinating story. In the instance of this NDE, there is no life review. As I previously mentioned, not all NDEs are identical as they may contain some variations.

Chapter 4

§

YOU ARE MORE THAN JUST A BODY - THE NDE OF DANNION BRINKLEY

*"You are not your body at all. Your body is something
that you have; it is not something that you are.
Who you are is limitless and without end."*

GOD-THROUGH-NEALE, THE NEW REVELATIONS:
A CONVERSATION WITH GOD

In this second case, we look at the NDE of Mr. Dannion Brinkley
as documented in his book *Saved by the Light*. This experience
takes place back on September 17,1975 when Dannion is speaking to his close friend Tommy over the telephone in the midst of
a thunder storm. The lightning strikes the phone line and he is
fatally electrocuted. The electrical shock is so intense that it melts
the phone in his hand. At first he's aware of the immense pain, but
then he suddenly finds himself floating above his body, engulfed

by peace and tranquility. His wife Sandy, who was home at the time of the accident, makes every effort to resuscitate Dannion, but there is little response.

Dannion's friend Tommy rushes over to the house because he had heard the explosion over the phone. An ambulance is called and both Sandy and Tommy accompany Dannion to the hospital. At this time, he recalls hovering above everyone as they ride through the rain to the hospital. As with many NDErs, he's able to empathize with all the people that he focuses on: his wife, his friend Tommy, and the paramedics attempting to revive him. He can actually feel exactly what they are feeling. He's completely aware as the paramedic removes the stethoscope from his body and says, "He's gone."

Now, when Dannion tells this story in his seminar, he recalls his thought when looking down at his traumatized body: "How did anyone ever convince me to get into that?" The other thought that comes to him is the realization that, "Who he was had nothing to do with that body they had just covered with a sheet."[31]

From here, Dannion begins to accept the reality that he is dead. He goes on to describe the sound of chimes and a tunnel spiraling toward and then around him. He goes through the tunnel that opens up into a paradise of the most brilliant light that he's ever seen. He is met by a beautiful being of light and senses that this magnificent and powerful being is emanating great love and compassion.

When Moody conducted his study on patients who had an NDE, he noted that this "Being of Light" is the single most common element across the cases he studied and it has the most profound effect upon the individual.[32]

Dannion attempts to describe the moment: *"Looking at this Being I had the feeling that no one could love me better, no one could have more empathy, sympathy, encouragement and nonjudgmental compassion for me than this Being."*

In this life review, as recorded in so many other life reviews, there are no words spoken. Rather, there is thought transference or telepathic communication between the Being of Light and Dannion.[33]

Another medical doctor Melvin Morse conducted his study of the NDE in children, as documented in his book *Closer to the Light*. In most of his case studies the children tell him about the Light:

"Describing the Light is difficult. Most of the patients I have spoken to describe it essentially as a pure light of unconditional love. Others call it "all-knowing," "all-forgiving," and "all-loving." One patient twenty years after seeing the Light at age five, told me, "I will never forget that Light."

"Children even draw pictures of the Light. In fact, when I ask children to draw pictures of what happened during their near death experience, they almost always include a representation of the Light.

It is fascinating to me that these children, sometimes as young as two and three years old, use the same descriptions of the Light as the previously mentioned spiritual leaders use in their descriptions of the Light of God."[34]

In the company of this Being of Light, Dannion has his life reviewed beginning with his early, angry, childhood through to his present adult years. The life review is not just about you; rather, you will have the opportunity to experience and relive not only your actions, emotions, and thoughts but also those emotions, sentiments, and thoughts of the people you affected. In Dannion's case, he also sees and relives his actions. He even sees how his actions affect others who are completely removed from the immediate activity. In New Age circles, this is sometimes referred to as the "ripple effect" because during the life review, the NDErs have the opportunity to see and experience the repercussions of their actions. This is similar to waves rippling outward when a stone is thrown into the still waters of a pond. Dannion is the first to admit that while growing up he was not the nicest person in the neighbourhood. He was constantly fighting in grade school and up through high school. He recalls that his grade school had a "demerit point" system. If you had fifteen demerits they would call in your parents. Kids who had thirty demerits were suspended from school. In the seventh grade, Dannion had received one hundred and fifty-four demerits by the third day of school - he grew up as a very angry and truculent kid. Dannion points out that today we have more tolerance and understand a lot more about kids like him, but back then they were just labeled "really bad kids". At that time in South Carolina they had racial segregation between blacks and whites and racial tensions were raw and ran high. Oftentimes Dannion would take part in organized race fights because he embraced the hate and enjoyed the conflict and violence. As he witnessed this in his life review, he says, *"I relived each one of those alterations, but with one major difference: I was the receiver. I wasn't the receiver in the sense that I felt the punches I had thrown. Rather, I felt the anguish and the humiliation my opponent felt."*[35]

He also saw firsthand how his actions had been extremely hurtful to his parents, even though they had tried to discipline him the very best they could. And if you think that the life review just pertains to people, think again. Cruelty to animals is a factor in Dannion's life review. He sees a time when he caught his dog chewing on the carpet and he removed his belt and beat the dog mercilessly without any consideration for an alternative form of discipline. Now, as he relives this moment in his life review, he feels the dog's love for him and could tell that the dog never meant to do what he was doing. In this moment, he's able to feel the dog's sorrow and pain. As a young man, Dannion joined the U.S. military as a combat soldier: the perfect outlet for his anger and aggression. Without going into the graphic details, he commits his most horrendous and brutal acts of violence - all dismissed as acts of war.[36] This life review is a time when we really have to see ourselves as we really are. There is no justifying or concealing misdeeds or the bad choices, decisions, and hurtful actions that we have caused another to experience. Once the life review is complete, Dannion describes his anxiety of acknowledging his less than perfect life:

> "When I finished the review, I arrived at a point of reflection in which I was able to look back on what I had just witnessed and come to a conclusion. I was ashamed. I realized I had led a very selfish life, rarely reaching out to help anyone. Almost never had I smiled as an act of brotherly love or just handed somebody a dollar because he was down and needed a boost. No, my life had been for me and me alone. I hadn't given a damn about my fellow humans."[37]

Not all of Dannion's life review was negative. Where he had done good things for himself and others, he felt those good feelings. That is, the good feeling that he had given to another came back to him in his life review. As I mentioned earlier, I went to hear Dannion speak in Toronto. Whenever he speaks, he always hangs out afterwards, patiently waiting to meet all of his listeners if need be. He offers a handshake or a warm hug and will gladly sign your book. He says that he does this because he now knows that the *"good feelings"* that he gives to you and me will ultimately come back to him in his next life review. Since his life review, he now re-alizes the importance of how you make another person feel. I think that it is imperative to understand the insights from Dannion's life review because it shows us all the real truth about who God is. Even when you and I live a less than stellar life, even when we're acting our worst and committing the most ungodly acts, there is no wrath, judgement, punishment, or condemnation from God. There is only unconditional love, unlimited compassion, and car-ing. Over and over again, the NDEers tell us that we are the ones who judge ourselves - you can't lie to yourself. Dannion summa-rizes his life review experience with these words:

> *"I looked at the Being of Light and felt a deep sense of sorrow and shame. I expected a rebuke, some kind of cosmic shaking of my soul. I had reviewed my life and what I had seen was a truly worthless person. What did I deserve if not a rebuke? As I gazed at the Being of Light I felt as though he was touching me: From that contact I felt a love and joy that could only be compared to the non-judgmental compassion that a grandfather has for a grandchild."* [38]

The life review is of no small consequence. In Neale's conversation with God, he questions God about the purpose of the life review. God explains that after we complete our time with the physical body and return to the spiritual realm, we will want a life review; we will ask for a life review. It is part of the process by which we come to know more about ourselves and about Life, by which we evolve in our spiritual growth.[39]

Chapter 5

YOU ARE MORE THAN JUST A BODY - THE NDE OF ANITA MOORJANI

"It is something that you are using. It is a tool. A device.
A mechanism that responds and reacts in particular
ways under particular influences and when subjected
to particular stimuli. This mechanism can be hurt or
damaged or destroyed, but "you" cannot. This tool can
be rendered completely inoperable, but you cannot.
This device can cease to function but you cannot."

GOD-THROUGH-NEALE, *THE NEW REVELATIONS:*
A CONVERSATION WITH GOD

M s. Anita Moorjani is a survivor of cancer after battling with the deadly disease for four agonizing years. On this fateful day, it appears that she has inevitably lost her fight. Anita is rushed to hospital in a deep coma brought about by advanced stage lymphoma, a cancer that attacks the body's lymphatic system. She remembers the date of February 2nd, 2006 because this, Anita will tell you, is the day that she died. Her husband Danny accompanies her to the hospital emergency unit, where a team of doctors are anxiously awaiting her arrival. Anita's eye witness account of her life, death, and decision to return to her physical body is well documented in her book entitled *Dying To Be Me*.[40]

In Anita's case, her essence begins to leave her body quite gradually. She is literally dying as she is rushed into the emergency unit of the hospital. Once the doctors take a look at Anita's physical appearance, they are convinced that it is too late to save her. Even though her five physical senses have all but shut down, Anita begins to experience a heightened awareness and a release from the suffering and tormenting pain. Like many NDErs, she watches on as a team of doctors and nurses work frantically to stabilize her deteriorating condition. Eventually Anita is moved into an intensive care unit and recalls her state of conscious awareness:

> *"I knew when people came in to see me, who they were and what they were doing. Although my physical eyes were closed, I seemed to be acutely aware of every minute detail that was taking place around me and beyond. The sharpness of my perception was even more intense than if I'd been awake and using my physical senses. I seemed to just know and understand everything - not only what was going on around me, but also what everyone was feeling, as though I were able to see and feel through each person. I was able to sense their fears, their hopelessness, and their resignation to my situation."*[41]

During this time, the doctor has taken Anita's husband Danny aside to tell him in a very straightforward manner the grim prognosis. He informs Danny that his wife's body is riddled with large tumours, her organs are failing, and her brain and lungs are filled with fluid. There is not much that they can do for Anita now. In her current condition, they don't expect Anita to make it through the night.[42]

In the meantime, Anita has already crossed over into the spiritual realm. As she is immersed in this new sense of peacefulness and tranquility, she begins to realize that she must be dying, but she is feeling better than she's ever felt before. This is a common occurrence with NDErs who have watched on calmly as their bodies are resuscitated or who have observed their lifeless bodies after leaving them temporarily. They don't think that they're dead because they feel more alive, light, and free than ever before. As Anita observes her limp body laying in the hospital bed she feels no emotional attachment to her body and she wonders how, in her present state of magnificence and grandeur, she could ever be housed in such a small body:

> *"The overwhelming sensations were in a realm of their own and words don't exist to describe them. The feeling of complete, pure, unconditional love was unlike anything I'd known before. Unqualified and non-judgmental....it was totally undiscriminating, as if I didn't have to do anything to deserve it, nor did I need to prove myself to earn it. In that state of clarity, I also realized that I'm not who I'd always thought I was: Here I am without my body, race, culture, religion or beliefs ... yet I continue to exist! Then what am I? Who am I? I certainly don't feel reduced or smaller in any way. On the contrary, I haven't ever been this*

*huge, this powerful, or this all encompassing. Wow, I've never,
ever felt this way!"* [43]

In the spiritual realm, there are no questions that cannot be answered. In our earthly lives, it can take considerable time to learn new concepts and understand the events in our lives, but in the spiritual realm there are no secrets. As quickly as you can formulate a question, it is answered thoroughly in a way that gives you all the details and a full and complete understanding in that very moment. As spiritual beings in the spiritual realm, there is nothing that is hidden from us. In Anita's case, she turns her attention to her brother Anoop and she sees him. In that moment, he's on an airplane flying to Hong Kong from India in the desperate hope of seeing his dying sister before she passes away. Now, in her present state, Anita not only sees her brother on the plane but is able to feel his fear, worry, and determination.

As she turns her focus on the last four years of her life of battling the cancer, the reason for her cancer becomes perfectly clear. Anita sees that her cancer is the result of her own thoughts and beliefs about herself: *"Just look at my life path! Why, oh why, have I always been so harsh with myself? Why was I always beating myself up? Why was I always forsaking myself? Why did I never stand up for myself and show the world the beauty of my own soul?"* [44]

Now, as she reflects upon her life, she realizes that she has not been true to herself. Oftentimes Anita was fearful to show her creativity and intelligence; she was always needing and seeking the approval of others and never following her own beautiful truth. She realizes also that the cancer was not a punishment for something she had done or hadn't done. It was not the result of bad karma, but simply the culmination of all her choices and decisions. Anita's many fears and great power had manifested the disease.[45]

Anita makes it very clear that negative thought is not necessarily the origin of all cancers. It would be wholly inaccurate to assume that all cancers are the result of our thoughts and beliefs. But each situation is different, and in Anita's case, she attributes the origins of her cancer to the thoughts and beliefs she held about herself. It is a well known fact that the medical community has known about the mind-body connection for several decades through its research into the "placebo effect". Without a doubt the placebo effect has shown that positive, life affirming thoughts strengthen our immune system, while negative life denying thoughts weaken our immune system. Some of the more progressive doctors treating cancer patients today use a number of unconventional therapies and activities designed to boost a patient's positive thoughts of themselves and uplift their self-esteem.[46] As Anita moves deeper into this spiritual realm, she encounters what she calls the essence of her father, who had died ten years earlier. She also meets the essence of her dearly missed friend Sonia, who had also died of cancer some three years prior. There is great joy and overwhelming love in this reunion and she comes to the understanding that they have always been with her throughout her lifetime and particularly during the last four years as she fought with the cancer. Eventually, her father cautions Anita that her work on earth is not yet complete, but she can stay if she chooses - she has a choice. However, she cannot venture any further into the spiritual realm until she makes a definite decision to stay. Again, in the communication between Anita and her father, there are no "words" spoken but rather there is a thought-transference: a common understanding between herself and her father. Given the current conditions of her cancer-stricken body and enduring the endless aches and pains, she decides that she wants to stay in the spiritual realm forever. She senses the reassurance that whatever she should decide, everything would work out to be okay. At that moment, she becomes conscious of her body dying, the intense grief of her distraught husband, and the doctors telling her family that her death was caused by organ failure brought about by advanced stage lymphoma. Just before she prepares to cross the final threshold, however, she receives this startling revelation:

> "In the moment that I made the decision to go on toward death, I became aware of a new level of truth. I discovered that since I'd realized who I really was and understood the magnificence of my true self, if I chose to go back to life, my body would heal rapidly - not in months or weeks, but in days! I knew that the doctors wouldn't be able to find a trace of cancer if I chose to go back into my body! How can that be? I was astounded by this revelation, and wanted to understand why. It was then that I understood that my body is only a reflection of my internal state. If my inner self were ware of its greatness and connection with All-that-is, my body would soon reflect that and heal rapidly."[47]

With this newfound realization of her true magnificence and god-liness, Anita finds new incentive to go on with her physical life. Before she returns from death's doorstep, Anita's father and Sonia give her one last, parting message. I think that their message is meant for all of us to hear. They communicate to Anita saying, *"Now that you know the truth of who you really are, go back and live your life fearlessly!"*[48]

Just as she had foreseen, while in the spiritual realm Anita returns to her body and begins a physical recovery that is nothing short of miraculous. In the morning Anita begins to open her eyes and her family is overjoyed to see her again. She recognizes her brother Anoop at her bedside, and to his astonishment tells him how she saw him coming over on the plane. Her doctors are completely shocked and astounded as they walk into the room and find her awake and talking.[49] Since that time, Anita has published her story in her own book *Dying to Be Me* - a book that has provided hope, healing, and spiritual support for millions of people around the world. Just recently, Anita has now come out with another new book entitled *"Deep Meditation for Healing"*, which explains how we can all take steps to heal ourselves.

Chapter 6

YOU ARE MORE THAN JUST A BODY - THE NDE OF DR. EBEN ALEXANDER

"You are not the conglomeration of bones and muscle and tissue and internal systems that you call your body. That is not Who You Are. Your body is yours, but it is not you."

GOD-THROUGH-NEALE, THE NEW REVELATIONS:
A CONVERSATION WITH GOD

All of the NDE cases reviewed so far have been nothing short of extraordinary and remarkable. The NDE of Dr. Eben Alexander, documented in his book entitled *Proof of Heaven: A Neurosurgeon's Journey into the Afterlife*, is of particular interest because it directly addresses the claims, made by the skeptics, that the NDE is nothing more than a "brain-based hallucination".

You see, of all the people who could possibly have an NDE, God chose Dr. Eben Alexander, a Harvard-trained neurosurgeon and researcher, to once again send us a clear message and remind us of who we really are. First, I think that it's imperative that we all understand where Eben is coming from. He describes his dedication and impeccable record in medical research and neurosurgery:

> *"Most of my research work involved the development of advanced technical procedures like stereotactic radiosurgery, a technique that allows surgeons to precisely guide beams of radiation to specific targets deep in the brain without affecting adjacent areas. I also helped develop magnetic resonance image-guided neurosurgical procedures instrumental in repairing hard-to-treat brain conditions like tumors and vascular disorders. During those years I also authored or coauthored more than 150 chapters and papers for peer-reviewed medical journals and presented my findings at more than two hundred medical conferences around the world. In short I devoted myself to science. Using the tools of modern medicine to help and to heal people, and to learn more about the workings of the human body and brain, was my life calling."*[50]

To really appreciate Eben's spiritual transformation, we have to remember that as a dedicated doctor who was immersed in research and working on the cutting-edge of medical science, Eben had never seriously contemplated the reality of the NDE. He's very open and honest about his own skepticism on such beliefs. Even though he had heard firsthand accounts from his own patients, he always thought that it was nothing more than fantasy, as he describes it:

"When your brain is absent, you are absent, too. As a neurosurgeon, I'd heard many stories over the years of people who had strange experiences, usually after suffering cardiac arrest: stories of travelling to mysterious, wonderful landscapes; of talking to dead relatives - even of meeting God himself. Wonderful stuff no question. But all of it, in my opinion, was pure fantasy. What caused the otherworldly types of experiences that such people so often report? I didn't claim to know, but I did know that they were brain-based. All of consciousness is. If you don't have a working brain, you can't be conscious."[51]

"Like an ocean wearing away a beach, over the years my scientific worldview gently but steadily undermined my ability to believe in something larger. Science seemed to be providing a steady onslaught of evidence that pushed our significance in the universe ever closer to zero. Belief would have been nice. But science is not concerned with what would be nice. It's concerned with what is."[52]

Eben's life is inevitably changed forever when he inexplicably and spontaneously contracts a case of E Coli bacterial meningitis, an extremely rare and potentially fatal condition that affects only one in ten million adults worldwide annually. This strain of meningitis is highly aggressive, and ninety percent of the people who experience this rapid neurological decline will die.

On the morning of November 10th, 2008, Eben is discovered by his wife Holly, lying in bed, in the midst of a full grand mal seizure. He's rushed to the Lynchburg General Hospital emergency room, where he slips into a deep coma for the next seven days. While the doctors are rushing about madly trying to diagnose Eben's condition and his wife and family are watching on anxiously, Eben quietly leaves his body and slips away into the spiritual realm.

When he first becomes conscious of his new surroundings, he becomes aware that he is in what seems to be a kind of under-world. This is a world that Eben describes as "visible darkness" - suffocating and claustrophobic. His surroundings are reminiscent of being deep under the ground. He becomes aware of a sound off in the distance - like the incessant pounding of a heavy metal hammer against an iron anvil - as he describes it. Understandably, the realm is unfamiliar and Eben begins to feel some anxiety and trepidation. If there is an unpleasant part of his journey, then this is it. Eben calls this realm the "Earthworm's Eye View" because he imagines that this is how an earthworm might see the world from its perspective.

This is not, by any means, a pleasant realm to be in, but before we confuse it with a trip to purgatory or worse yet to the dreaded realms of eternal darkness and damnation, it should be made clear that during this time Eben never senses a great evil nor is he aware of the presence of any dark, demonic forces while he is there. The realm of the "Earthworm's Eye View" is simply not a nice place to be. Like being stranded outside, at night, in a cold, damp rain, there's nothing evil or demonic about this place; it's just a very uncomfortable place to be. As he begins to think about getting out and getting away from this earthworm perspective, he becomes aware of a beautiful, spiraling light piercing through the muddy darkness, opening up and coming towards him. Not only does he witness the alluring light, but he becomes aware of rich and exquisite music accompanying the light. Before he knows it, he is engulfed by the light and finds himself moving up and rapidly through it. Eventually, he finds himself literally flung into a whole new world of unspeakable beauty and brilliance:[53]

> "There was a whooshing sound, and in a flash I went through the opening and found myself in a completely new world. The strangest, most beautiful world I'd ever seen. Brilliant, vibrant, ecstatic, stunning ... I could heap on one adjective after another to describe what this world looked and felt like, but they'd all fall short. I felt like I was being born. Not reborn, or born again. Just...born. Below me there was countryside. It was green, lush, and earth-like. It was earth... but at the same time it wasn't. It was like when your parents take you back to a place where you spent some years as a very young child. You don't know the place. Or at least you think you don't but as you look around, something pulls at you, and you realize that a part of yourself, a part way, deep down - does remember the place after all, and it is rejoicing at being back there again."[54]

Eben finds himself flying over this beautiful and wondrous countryside looking down at fields, streams, waterfalls, and occasionally people. He sees children laughing and playing and people singing, dancing, and rejoicing. He becomes aware of a presence that is flying along with him, by his side. Eben describes her as a beautiful female companion or guide who is helping him to navigate through this new world.

Now, if you read Eben's full description in *Proof of Heaven* you may be inclined to say that he's having a wonderful dream, but if anyone is qualified to differentiate between fantasy and reality, I would say that a skeptical, highly trained neurosurgeon such as Eben would be the best judge of that. He's adamant that this otherworldly experience is even more real than his current earthly life - a fact that he still maintains to this very day. Eben refers to this beautiful countryside and its inhabitants as "The Gateway". Later he comes to realize that his lovely companion who accompanies him throughout his journey is really acting as an interpreter between himself and God. Like other NDErs who have visited the spiritual realm, although no words are spoken, all questions are answered through thought transference. Eben describes the first communication between himself and his companion as a message that could only come from a God of infinite love and compassion: [55]

> "Without using any words, she spoke to me. The message went through me like a wind, and I instantly understood that it was true. I knew so in the same way that I knew that the world around us was real - was not some fantasy, passing and insubstantial. The message had three parts, and if I had to translate them into earthly language, I'd say they ran something like this: "You are loved and cherished, dearly, forever.", "You have nothing to fear.", "There is nothing you can do wrong." [56]

From here Eben is guided to a third realm that he refers to as "The Core". It is here that Eben communes with God, not just by having all of his questions answered but he's also given deep, spiritual insights into the workings of life and the living universe. He learns that there are actually many universes, many spiritual beings, and that only a very small portion of evil is permitted to allow us to exercise free will.

Eventually, Eben goes back to the realm of the earthworm's eye view, but now there is no anxiety or fear because he has a greater awareness of his true power. He learns that by directing his thoughts and will alone, he's able to move effortlessly between the three realms. As some point, he surmises that he is being given a kind of tour of the spiritual realm: a tour that shows the good and not so good levels in the spiritual realm.

The other unique aspect of Eben's NDE is the complete amnesia of his identity and his personal life. While on this journey he has completely forgotten that he is a loving husband, father, and doctor. He meets no beloved deceased family members or friends like Anita or Mary did. In hindsight, he understands that this was necessary for him, so he could fully absorb the experience without any distraction.

Meantime, back in the earthly realm, Eben's doctors are completely dumbfounded that Eben's physical condition remains unchanged. He not responding to the antibiotics, and they believe that the longer he remains in a coma, the less likely he will ever make a full recovery and lead a relatively normal life again. The doctor assigned to Eben's case schedules a meeting with Eben's wife Holly to discuss his condition and give her his personal medical opinion. The doctor knows that seven days is an extremely long time for a person to be in a coma with bacterial meningitis. Even if, by some miracle, Eben should return from this coma, his quality of life may entail undue suffering for both Eben and his family. The doctor makes no direct recommendation, but in his tone and demeanor he is implying that it may be better to let Eben die. It would appear that Eben's story ends here, but eventually he is returned to his body and does something that defies all medical explanation - he comes back from a seven-day coma with a full blown case of bacterial meningitis and makes a full recovery![57]

After spending the equivalent of seven earthly days in the spiritual realm, what do you think is the most significant and sincere message that Eben brings back to us? Care to take a guess...? Eben comes back with the same message that we've already heard from Dannion, Mary, and Anita. Eben's message is this:

"The unconditional love and acceptance that I experienced on my journey is the single most important discovery I have ever made, or will ever make, and as hard as I know it's going to be to unpack the other lessons I learned while there, I also know in my heart that sharing this very basic message - one so simple that most children readily accept it - is the most important task I have."[58]

Coming back from the NDE, Eben now faces a struggle that many of us have had or will have in our lives: attempting to reconcile what we've been told and what we believe about God and life versus our own personal life experience.

Without question, these NDE eyewitness accounts give consistent testimony for a God of unconditional love and compassion. In the next three chapters we'll look at why and how we're unable to believe in a God of unconditional love.

Chapter 7

GOD IS STILL TALKING TO US

*"God has never stopped communicating directly
with human beings. God has been communicating
with and through human beings from the
beginning of time. God does so today."*

God-through-Neale, The New Revelations:
A Conversation with God

My skeptical friends will look at these NDEs and say, "Those people weren't really dead, they were all still alive" - and you know what? They're right! However, they are only reinforcing what our spiritual masters and great prophets have been telling us for over two thousand years: There is no death! Death is not an end, but a new beginning. Not a closing down, but an opening up. As one NDEr said to the skeptic, "When you die, you're in for the biggest surprise party of your life!" Given the abundant amount of documented NDE cases, reliable eyewitness accounts, and ancient teachings of our spiritual masters, do you really believe that the near-death experience is reserved for only a select few? This is the experience that you and I will have some day. God did not stop talking to us two thousand years ago.

The other day, my thirteen-year-old youngest daughter told me a funny joke that I have to share with you now. Once there was an avid sailor who wanted to sail his boat across the Caribbean Sea. He got caught in a fierce storm and his boat capsized into the water, throwing him and many of his belongings into the sea. Miraculously he managed to swim through the high waves back to his capsized boat which was still afloat in the water. He clung to the capsized boat for dear life, and eventually managed to pull himself on top. Being a man of great faith and religious dedication, he was positive that God would save him. He prayed faithfully for God to intervene and rescue him from his plight, but he received no answer from God. Later that day, another boat came by and the sailor on board asked him if he needed any help. Sitting on top of his overturned boat, he replied, "No, I'll be okay - help is already on its way." Then six hours later, a family came by in a luxury yacht and offered the man assistance. He declined their help, fully convinced and self-assured that God would rescue him at any moment. Nightfall came and the man spent the entire night sitting atop his overturned boat praying and waiting patiently for God. The next morning a fishing vessel passed by and the fisherman threw a rope to the stranded man, but he stuck to his belief and ignored the rope. He told the fishermen that he was confident of his rescue and there was no need to worry. Later that same day, another violent storm set in and this time the man was not so lucky. The storm sank the boat and the man soon drowned in the turbulent waters. His spirit ascended to Heaven and his first question to God was, "I've always been a great believer and faithful servant; why didn't you rescue me when I asked?" God replied, "I sent you three boats." The principle behind this story is that God can talk to us in so many different ways. God is not talking to us using only "words". God talks to us through our thoughts and feelings, but his greatest tool of enunciation is experience. If we really want to know what God is saying to us, we have to listen to our experience.[59] God is always our highest thought, and our grandest vision of who we are. God is still talking to us today through the NDEs of Anita, Eben, Neale, Helen, Mary, Dannion, and the many other NDErs and messengers who have told their story and brought their message.

It is a time for us to rejoice and celebrate in our deeper understanding of God and the true nature of who we really are! Our bodies and our lives will pass away, but we never pass away - we are immortal. There are several spiritual truths that emerge from the study of NDEs, but for me, there are two predominant truths that distinguish themselves - two spiritual truths that stand out. First, the God I learned about of judgment, wrath, and vengeance simply does not exist - this is a total misconception of who and what God is. This magnificent and wonderful, supreme creator of Heaven and Earth that you and I may refer to as God, Allah, Jehovah, Krishna, Jah, Lord, Yahweh, Most High, etc... has unconditional, unlimited love and compassion for all of us. The second prominent spiritual truth is that we are all Gods and will never ever die. In our truest, most genuine essence, we are Gods and Goddesses - that is who we really are and we are nothing short of that! Our survival is never in question; it is only a question of which form we are going to take. Will we be in our familiar bodily form, or will we be in our divine spiritual form? We may think that life is a constant battle and "only the strong survive", or we may feel that life is an ongoing struggle and it's "survival of the fittest". Well, here's the good news: everybody survives!

> *"Yet I tell you this: My love is unlimited and unconditional. This is the one thing you cannot hear, the one truth you cannot abide, the one statement you cannot accept, for its all inclusiveness destroys not only the institution of marriage (as you have constructed it), but every one of your religions and governmental institutions as well. For you have created a culture based on exclusion and sup-ported it with a cultural myth of a God who excludes. Yet the cul-ture of God is based on inclusion. In God's love, everyone is includ-ed. Into God's Kingdom everyone is invited. And this truth is what you call a blasphemy."[60]*

God-through-Neale

As Anita was saying, when we are stripped of our culture, race, family ties, livelihood, physical possessions, beliefs, and even our physical bodies, all that is left is our pure, divine, magnificent, spiritual essence. When we complete this lifetime and our physi-cal body dies, we will continue to live forever! In that moment, we will know the deep peace, tranquility, and unbridled joy in our release from the physical body. We will be completely free of physical pain and heartache. Every question we ever asked will be answered. We'll immediately understand the larger picture be-hind our earthly trials and struggles we endured in life. We will communicate through thought, without the awful limitation of words. We will be able to empathize with any person we wish. We will experience total awareness. We will be able to move anywhere with the speed of our thought. We will gaze in awe and wonderment at the indescribable beauty and brilliance of the spiritual realm and we will finally know the unlimited and unconditional love of God.

"Have I not said that ye are gods?"[61]

God-through-Neale

Given your life experience and current beliefs, you may think that I'm a religious fanatic just promoting a lot of spiritual "fluff" or just trying to make you feel good. Perhaps you think that these ideas are totally preposterous, but the overwhelming evidence shows that they are absolutely true: this is who and what we really are - nothing less than Gods and Goddesses in an ongoing spiritual journey. If it were up to me, that is, if I could decide what you should take from this reading, it would be these two spiritual truths. I want to convey this message because we live in a world where we are made to feel little and powerless.

A GOD OF UNCONDITIONAL AND UNLIMITED LOVE

If you truthfully contemplate your life, you'll see that there are not very many real instances of sincere, unconditional love. This is something that we rarely get to experience while we're going about our earthly lives. During our lifetime, we may experience many personal relationships that appear to be genuine, loving, and caring. However, the harsh reality is that many of us have all kinds of conditions around our love. When adverse circumstances or conditions bring a change in our lives, such as infamy, emotional/

physical challenges, poor health, addiction or economic hardship, a so-called "loving relationship" can change very quickly. We, especially in the West, have become so materialistic and shallow that too often we can only give our love depending on who a person is or what a person has or what a person does. If there's one source of love that may endure through our most difficult trials and struggles, it is a mother's love for her children. Yet it doesn't take much imagination to see that even a good mother will withhold or deny her love under certain circumstances and conditions. Our NDErs, however, give resounding testimony to the deep and unparalleled unconditional love of God.

"You cannot understand how much your Father loves you, for there is no parallel in your experience of the world to help you understand it. There is nothing on earth with which it can compare and nothing you have ever felt apart from him resembles it ever so faintly."[62]

God-through-Helen (ACIM, T-14.IV.8:4,5)

I understand completely that many of us cannot accept the idea of a God of unconditional love - I completely understand that. After all, we have been thoroughly conditioned by our religions and parents that God is a menacing, intolerable God who demands perfection, obedience, and strict adherence to certain religious laws and doctrines. We are brought up in a world where our behaviours that are perceived as good are rewarded, and our behaviours that are perceived as bad are punished. Reward and punishment is a social construct of earthly life, but it is not a construct of God's world. You can't have unlimited and unconditional love in the same space as reward and punishment.

For me, living with the knowledge of a God of unlimited and unconditional love changed everything! First and foremost, I have no more fear of God. At one time, I would have described myself as a "God-fearing man", but not anymore. Now, I am a "God-loving man". Unconditional love means that regardless of race, gender, nationality, religious persuasion, sexual orientation, or any other aspect of a person's individuality, we are fully entitled to the love of God, and, as Anita asserts, we don't have to do anything to "earn" it.

PORTRAIT OF AN ANGRY GOD

At this point, you may be asking yourself: "If God is not an angry and vengeful God, then how can it be that so much of our religious teachings and holy scriptures tell us about an angry, vengeful God?" In Neale's conversation with God, he poses just this question. God explains that it all started when we, as the earliest humans - going back to the caveman era - tried to make sense of and find reason behind the "bad things" that happened in our lives.

In primitive times, we witnessed naturally occurring earthly events such as thunder and lightning, hurricanes and tornadoes, violent earthquakes, massive waves upon the ocean, and forest fires that started mysteriously by themselves. From time to time, we had to endure catastrophic episodes of famine, drought, pestilence, and disease that came along and wiped out everything. We didn't understand why people died or why these things happened at all. In fact, early humans were completely ignorant of the reasons behind these naturally occurring events - they had no understanding of seasonal weather patterns or seismic activity. In trying to make sense of this, we reasoned that there was something out there that was bigger and more powerful than ourselves. We began to believe that this "other thing" was responsible for causing this adversity in our lives. We arrived at the belief that this "other thing" committed these acts based on mood and whim, and that we must do certain things to affect that mood and whim. We began to deify nature, creating a Sun God, a Rain God, and a host of other Gods that we believed were responsible for our lives and our problems. Over time we created many rituals and rites of passage, such as rites of fertility in order to call forth the spirit of these Gods and meet the approval of these Gods. Today we would refer to some of these rituals as pagan customs. The worship of idols was a common practice of many early religions. Eventually stories were told about how heavenly Gods would directly influence life on earth and how life on earth could directly influence heavenly Gods. These frequently told stories became myths, which turned into beliefs and became "true" for a great many people. As these myths turned into truths, they became the earliest foundations of our organized religions. As our religions grew, they had to compete to obtain and retain members. They found that fear was a great tool that could be used to control their members, and this fear is still used today. The idea of an angry, vengeful God that required obedience and perfection was perfect for controlling the masses and helped to increase and retain the membership.[63]

Today, it's very easy to see how early humans could have come to these beliefs. If we look around ourselves today, we still continue to see these ancient remnants of belief in a God of wrath and vengeance. All of our major religions have preserved various rituals and rites of passage that, we believe, will please and satisfy a needy God. In addition, we continue to believe that God is behind the misfortune in our lives. For example, when the AIDS epidemic hit North America, many of our major religions jumped at the opportunity to declare that the epidemic was the act of an angry God - a God intolerant of the gay community and same sex partnerships. Oddly enough, our religions did not take this stance with the West Nile Virus nor the SARS outbreak in Toronto, Canada, back in February 2003. I personally know of conservative Christians who watched on stoically as Hurricane Katrina devastated New Orleans back in 2005 and actually believed that God had brought his wrath and intolerance against this "city of sin" - as if New Orleans has less morality than any other large, major city in the world. Even today our insurance companies are still very specific in their policies that they do not cover "acts of God" - those bad, naturally occurring events that happen to all of us.

One religious historian, Karen Armstrong, is a former Catholic nun turned author who writes extensively on the historic origins of religion and their impact on our lives. In her very popular book entitled *A History of God*, Karen tells us that in their earliest beginnings, our religions consisted of a number of crude rites and rituals that, in addition to idol worship, included the frequent offering up of animals and sometimes humans for a bloody sacrifice at the altar. All of this was done in order to placate and appease whatever God they happened to be worshipping. When we trace back to the historical origins of our religions, they've become more refined over the centuries. However, in light of what we know about God today, it becomes clearly evident that many of our organized religions are man-made creations, promoting an inaccurate story of God and our relationship to God.

Consider this: My family and I make our home in Southern Ontario, Canada. We frequently experience thunder and lightning storms into the spring and summer seasons. If I were to move the family to Northern Ontario, then I could expect the winter to last longer with colder temperatures and heavier snowfall. If we were to move to Vancouver, British Columbia, the winters would be milder and the spring would come earlier, but there would be a lot more rainfall than in Southern Ontario. If we lived along the Gulf of Mexico, there's a good chance we would be the victims of a fierce tropical storm or hurricane between the months of June through November. The different seasons and weather patterns in these locations are not the work of an angry God; we know now that these are just naturally occurring conditions in our environment which are dependent on various geographical locations on the Earth. Likewise, if you're an inhabitant of the planet Earth, then depending on your geographical location, you may be subjected to floods, earthquakes, thunderstorms, forest fires, hurricanes, disease, famine, drought, and pestilence - it all depends on where you make your home. We mustn't forget our environmentalists and ecologists either, who have been telling us for decades that we are the ones who are contributing, through global warming and pollution, to the vicious and powerful weather patterns that we are experiencing today.

Looking back on my own life on this Earth, I know that I've made many wrong choices and decisions - no doubt about it. If there exists an angry God, then some of those bad choices and decisions would have surely made God very angry. However, that has not been my life experience. Yes, I've made bad choices and decisions and suffered the consequences of those bad choices, but that is not the wrath of God. That is just me experiencing the consequences of my own creation.

It just goes to show that, since ancient times, we haven't come that far in our beliefs about God. Despite a growing awareness of our earthly environment, we still hold steadfast to archaic and inaccurate beliefs that are thousands and thousands of years old. Growing up in the Christian religion, this was a religious teaching that was drilled into us from an early age. God needed and wanted our obedience and our gratefulness or else. Well, "needs" and "requirements" go against any thought of an unconditional love. You can't love someone unconditionally and still require things from them - the two ideas are incompatible. Even the most conservative, orthodox, religious fundamentalist will accept the belief of "free will". I believe that free will is our greatest gift from God, but how can God have requirements when we've been given free will? God gives us free will to choose, but then becomes angry when we select a different choice? I don't believe that God has any requirements of us. Again, this is a throw-back to ancient times. There are certainly people out there who will demand requirements of us on God's behalf, but I don't believe that God himself has any requirements of us. This is what led me to my next realization of God: you can't hurt, damage, or offend God. As a spiritual being given absolute free will, I don't believe that there is something that I can do to hurt, damage, or offend God.

"My wonderful children, you are never not in my good graces. You have created in your imaginings a God whose feelings get hurt. My feelings do not get hurt. My sensitivities do not become offended. You cannot upset Me. You cannot make Me angry. Upset and anger are the very antithesis of Who and What I Am. You imagine that I am a Being like you, only bigger and more

powerful, living somewhere in the universe – some kind of parent figure with ego needs and emotional agitations that match your own.

Yet I tell you, that is not who and what I am."[64]

God-through-Neale

Anita, Dannion, Eben, and Mary were all physically pushed over the edge - ushered in through death's doorstep. In each experience, they endured extreme physical trauma, but once they were released from their bodies and returned to their spiritual form, there was never any pain, suffering, or emotional heartache. Despite the tragic circumstances that brought them to death, they experienced that they had never been hurt, damaged, or offended in any way whatsoever. On the contrary, they all struggle with words to tell us about the exquisite feeling of grandeur and unbridled joy in that moment - no earthly feeling even comes close. You and I will experience this also one day, when we complete our time on Earth. We will come to realize that we have never really been hurt or damaged in any way either.

Later on, in the chapters that follow we will look more closely at what our scientists are saying about God and life. For now, I can tell you this much: the theory of "Intelligent Design" or "Creationism" purports that the universe, including you, me, and everything in it, is the product of intentional, intelligent, creation as opposed to being a completely haphazard random event of nature. Currently, many of our best and brightest scientists, both past and present, support the idea of intelligent design. Not only that, but this support is gaining more momentum every year. Recently, a popular Canadian periodical, *Maclean's Magazine* dedicated an issue to *"Why so many people - including scientists - suddenly believe in an afterlife"*. In a nutshell, these scientists have come to the conclusion through their work that there is a benevolent, super, intelligence - call it God, Allah, or whatever you'd like - that creates universes. In Eben's NDE he says explicitly that during his communion with God, he was made aware of the existence of multiple universes that had been created by God.[65] The creation of universes is beyond the imagination, let alone comprehension. We have no words to truly describe those abilities which are immeasurable in their level of creativity and power. We may believe that there are certain things we can do from our position here on earth to hurt God or somehow damage or offend God, but it's a delusion and we are only fooling ourselves. Had we known this, if we'd acquired this understanding as early humans, we would never have seen the persistent patterns of warring and killing in the name of God throughout human history.

> *"There is no greater power in the world. The world was made by it, and even now depends on nothing else. The lessons you have taught yourself have been so overlearned and fixed they rise like heavy curtains to obscure the simple and the obvious."*[66]

> *God-Through-Helen (ACIM, T-31.I.3:2-4)*

Almost every believer in God will agree that God is all-powerful. The ultimate test of "all-powerful" is the invincibility from being hurt, damaged, or offended by anything or anybody in any way at any time. To be truly all-powerful, you would have no needs or requirements either. This, simply put, is the awesome and indescribable power of God.

Chapter 8

THE GOD IN YOU

"Some people call this glow the Light, the Eternal Flame, the Source, the Soul, or by other names that suit their particular poetry. It is, in fact, the Prime Essence, the Base Substance, the Core Material of all things. This Light is Who You Are."

GOD-THROUGH-NEALE, *THE NEW REVELATIONS: A CONVERSATION WITH GOD*

As gods and goddesses walking this earth, we are constantly inundated with messages from every possible source and direction - messages that tell us we are not gods and goddesses at all, but something significantly less than that. These messages come from our parents, our friends, our teachers, our spouses, our partners, our religions, the media, and society in general, but much worse than any of these are the messages that we give to ourselves - the ongoing, incessant, conversations that we have with ourselves every day. This is an insidious, internal dialogue that supports and promotes our own notions of being less than worthy of God's love or inferior.

As is common with many NDErs, after the experience Dannion Brinkley finds himself with enhanced psychic abilities. More specifically, he's able to hear people's thoughts and pick up on their self-impressions as documented in his book *At Peace in the Light*. Shortly after he comes out of the hospital, Dannion wants to get out of the house to avoid some of the boredom of being cooped-up all day. He goes out with a friend on a short trip to the local grocery store. While his friend ventures into the grocery store, Dannion waits quietly in the car, watching the shoppers going in and out of the store. His newly enhanced psychic abilities are tuned into the unsuspecting shoppers. Dannion describes the thoughts he's hearing:

"I was amazed by how negatively people viewed themselves. I still am. Beginning in those early days, it became clear to me that most people have a very low opinion of themselves. As I watched people go in and out of the store, I could hear their self-impressions. Most of their feelings were negative. They all seemed to feel guilty about some thing or another that they had done in their lives. Many felt they had done wrong things in their lives or that life had beaten them down so much that they felt inferior. I could tell that they never allowed themselves to touch themselves spiritually. Instead they focused on the surface things in their lives and picked themselves apart. Person after person, I could hear them think that they were ugly, overweight, or poor or bad parents, or

just downright dumb. I sure hope shopping doesn't do that to everyone, I thought."

"Rarely did the people whose thoughts I was picking up focus on what great and powerful spiritual beings they were. Few took credit for their greatness. I began to realize that people have almost a need to feel guilty, wrong, or inferior, and that this need seems to overwhelm any consideration that they are spiritual beings."[67]

The media, particularly the advertising media, sends out a constant barrage of messages telling us that if we don't have a certain something or don't get a certain something, then we're nobody - we're nothing. As we grow older, we become more secure with ourselves and our lifestyles and we are less susceptible to the media messages - but by that time, they've already beaten us down. Our young people especially are extremely vulnerable and impressionable when it comes to media advertising. When I was back in grade school and high school, we got teased and put down because we didn't have the right brand of blue jeans. At work bosses and coworkers routinely call into question our worth and significance to the company. We've created a society where it becomes very easy to look down on one's self, see only the shortcomings, and forget our magnificent, divine spirit.

"In this world, you believe you are sustained by everything but God. Your faith is placed in the most trivial and insane symbols; pills, money, "protective" clothing, influence, prestige, being liked, knowing the "right" people, and an endless list of forms of nothingness that you endow with magical powers."[68]

God-through-Helen (ACIM, W-P1.50.1:2,3)

It's not God's intention for us to feel small and insignificant. A part of God lives inside each of us and we must recognize our own true grandeur.

> *"Every thought of your Self as smaller than you really are is a denial of Me. Every word about your Self that puts you down is a denial of Me. Every action flowing through your Self that plays out a role of "not-good-enough", or lack, or insufficiency of any kind, is a denial indeed. Not just in thought, not just in word, but in deed. Do not allow your life to represent anything but the grandest version of the greatest vision you ever had about Who You Are.*[69]

God-Through-Neale

THE FALLACY OF ORIGINAL SIN

In Christianity, there is the ancient, age-old doctrine of "Original Sin". This doctrine claims that we are all inherent sinners. We are born in sin, and unless we take the appropriate steps, we will die as the lowly, pitiful, unrepentant sinners that we are. Not all of our major religions follow a doctrine of original sin, but they promote similar doctrines that portray us as imperfect and unworthy souls who are separate from God and undeserving of God's love and attention. These doctrines only serve to diminish our self-esteem and play down any grand ideas we may have about our divine, spiritual magnificence.

The late Elizabeth Clare Prophet (April 8th, 1939 - October 15th, 2009) was known in America as a New Age Minister and founder of the "Church Universal and Triumphant." She wrote extensively about religion, but unlike many Christian ministers she chose to write about the long forgotten Christian teachings that were a part of Christianity in its earliest beginning. These long forgotten teachings were subsequently repressed and replaced by the early church for teachings that were more agreeable and pleasing to the mandate of the Church - a mandate to act as the exclusive intermediary between God and humanity[70]. In her book entitled *Reincarnation - The Missing Link in Christianity*,[71] Prophet reveals how the idea of "original sin" was created, accepted, and promoted through the Church. Her work is corroborated by another religious historian and writer, Karen Armstrong, in *A History of God*.[72] This doctrine of "original sin" became a cornerstone of Christian theology and has only served to pervade all Christians with the blight of guilt, shame, and condemnation for thousands of years.

So how did Christians come to this idea of original sin? Although the thought of "original sin" did not originate from Saint Augustine, he became a defender and strong proponent of this Christian doctrine. Both Prophet and Armstrong tell us that Augustine was initially a theologian and philosopher who converted to Christianity and became bishop of the North African seaport of Hippo Regius - known today as Annaba, Algeria. At the time he was known as "Augustine of Hippo", but after his death, he was canonized by the Church and named Saint Augustine or Saint Austin (c. 354 - c. 430).[73]

Prophet contends that "Augustine's take on sex has also left a deep mark on our civilization. He, more than anyone else, was responsible for the idea that sex is inherently evil. He called it the most visible indication of man's fallen state." Dr. Elaine Pagel, a Professor of Religion, as Princeton University, reveals that Augustine saw sexual desire as "proof" and "penalty" for original sin. He even took the extreme view that sex, even in marriage, was evil.[74] The Church viewed the sexual act as evil because in the abandon of passionate lovemaking, the couple turned their attention away from God and all things holy, and instead focused their attention on each other - leaving God entirely out of the picture. Armstrong tells us that Augustine referred to this impassioned love-making as "concupiscence" – an irrational desire to take pleasure in mere creatures instead of God.[75] Augustine's reasoning goes all the way back to the time of Adam and Eve. It was Augustine's view that Adam would never have died, had he not eaten of the forbidden fruit. Adam's punishment was not only to grow old and die, but to experience uncontrollable lust. Sexual desire was thus the direct result of his fall. Augustine went further to conclude that because of Adam's sin, going forward, the entire human race would be bound for Hell and damnation, unless and only unless you managed to access God's grace through the Church. Augustine wrote, "We all were in that one man. Even though we didn't yet have physical form, already the seminal nature was there from which we were to be propagated." Augustine implies that the seeds of all humanity were contained in Adam's sperm. Prophet points out that Augustine also found support for his argument from holy scripture (Romans 5:12). In the modern New Revised Standard translation, the verse reads: "Sin came into the world through one man, and death came through sin, and so death spread to all because all have sinned. In this line of reasoning, even newborn babies were inherent sinners because they were brought into the world through a sinful act. Augustine warned that unless newborn babies were baptized, they were headed for eternal damnation.[76]

Today, the concept of reincarnation of the soul or previous existence of the soul is frequently categorized as New Age Theology, but these concepts are not new at all. Theologies built around reincarnation and previous existence of the soul flourished when Jesus walked the earth and for hundreds of years after Jesus left the earth[77]. The theology of reincarnation and previous existence of the soul created a problem for the early Church. After all, the mandate of the Church was to act as the single exclusive intermediary between God and humanity. Here we had the reincarnationists claiming that we should live our life to the best of our abilities and if we make mistakes, not to worry, we'll have another chance to get it right and another chance after that. With this belief in reincarnation and previous existence of the soul, people could bypass the Church altogether. No longer would they have to go to Church to stay in God's good graces or seek forgiveness for their sins through the Church. Clearly, this was a theology that would undermine the authority of the Church and thwart its political strategy. Understand too that this was a tumultuous time for the early Church because it had not yet solidified which teachings it would keep and which ones would be discarded as heretical.[78]

Great debates ensued, pitting various factions of the Church against itself as it attempted to consolidate these different theologies into one cohesive, comprehensible set of doctrines. At the time, there were other Bishops in the Church, just as there are people today, who thought that Augustine's idea of original sin was absurd. They argued that the entire human race could not be held responsible for the sins of Adam and a good and just God would never condemn an innocent, newborn baby to Hell. Prophet goes on to say that one of Augustine's chief opponents was a British theologian named Pelagius (c.354 - c.418). Early in c.417,

Augustine convinced Pope Innocent I "and Honorius, emperor of the western half of the empire, to excommunicate Pelagius (who lived in Rome) and send him into exile, along with his followers. Pelagius died soon after."[79] Augustine agreed that God was indeed good and just and would not bring harm to a newborn baby, but he countered with the argument that babies are born with physical and mental challenges and deformities which proved that the sins of the parents had been passed on to the newly born. If not, then God was not good and just and was responsible for infants suffering this "evil in the body"[80]. Supporters of reincarnation and previous existence of the soul shot back with their argument that infant suffering was a manifestation of previous sins committed in another time. Subsequently, these arguments, from the supporters of reincarnation, were stifled because they were seen as too detrimental to the authority of the early Church.

Augustine was not only the force behind original sin, but through his writings, he promoted a loathing and disrespect for women as well. He viewed all women as "the evil temptress" responsible for Adam's fall from grace. Armstrong writes: "Western Christianity never really recovered from this neurotic misogyny, which can still be seen in the unbalanced reaction to the very notion of the ordination of women."[81] It should be mentioned also, that the idea of a male God came about because, from our earliest beliefs, men saw themselves as stronger, more powerful and therefore superior to women. Yet through Neale's conversation with God, God makes it quite clear that God is an intelligent energy force in the universe and possesses traits of both male and female. As a great many women will attest, once we label God as a male, we place inherent limitations and restrictions on God and we cannot limit or restrict God.

So eventually Augustine won out and persuaded the early Church to accept the doctrine of original sin. He was successful in this quest for two reasons: First, he's the only one who could come up with an explanation of why infants were born with physical and mental challenges, and Augustine's explanation did not conflict with the early Church[82]. By the way, today we now understand why some of us are born with various challenges. This will be explained later. Second, this doctrine would serve to fortify the Church's authority as the exclusive intermediary between God and humanity. With the teachings of original sin promoted through the Church, every mother would want to ensure that her newborn baby was baptized, and, as is the case with many churches today, you had to be a member of the Church to have your baby baptized there. The tenet of original sin would be a windfall for the early church resulting in a burgeoning membership and overflowing coffers.

As I mentioned earlier, not all of our religions accept the teachings of Original Sin, but they all have their own teachings that - to say the least - marginalize our dignity and give rise to one's feelings of worthlessness, insignificance, and separation from God. Today some Christian religions have relented somewhat in their presumption regarding unbaptized babies. Now the unbaptized babies are not bound for eternal damnation, but are sent to "limbo" - a place that is not good nor bad but rather separate and away from God. Given the time and circumstances, I think that Saint Augustine was doing the best that he could for the early Church. I think that he was true to his beliefs at the time, but bless his heart - Saint Augustine was mistaken. Given what we know today about God and life, there is no original sin. Any idea of "original sin" comes with the arrogant thought that God would and could make inferior beings, as is the idea that women are somehow inferior to men or less than men in the eyes of God.

I'm discussing the history behind original sin to show that this idea came about through the misunderstanding and the erroneous reasoning of men in the early church. We are not original sinners and never have been. This was only how men, in the early church, imagined and wanted it to be. Original sin is just an idea that many of us accepted and came to believe in. However, nothing could be further from the truth:

> *"In the creation, God extended himself to his creations and imbued them with the same loving will to create. You have not only been fully created, but have also been created perfect. There is no emptiness in you."*[83]

> *God-through-Helen (ACIM, T-2.I.1:2-4)*

You might think to yourself, "Hold on here just a moment…did he just imply that I'm perfect? Are you trying to tell me that I'm created perfect?" The answer is emphatically "yes" - absolutely and without a doubt. If we look at ourselves from an earthly viewpoint, then we're inclined to find faults and deficiencies; but when you look at yourself from a spiritual standpoint, then we can see the perfection.

In my own, humble opinion, I would say that we cannot presume to fully understand God's entire plan for us here and now, but I sincerely believe that we are now catching a glimpse of that plan for you and me. Thanks to the NDE, the contemporary and ancient messengers of God, the gifted clairvoyants, and the courageous scientists and doctors, a clear pattern is taking shape. An undeniable message is beginning to emerge: this lifetime is for our learning and experiencing, which ultimately leads to our spiritual growth and higher consciousness. We are all on an incredible spiritual journey that will take us from being just good Gods to great Gods.

Imagine this, if you will: You are a loving parent of a healthy, newborn baby. Even before your healthy baby is born, grows into a toddler, and begins to walk, you already know, as a parent, that your little toddler will experience falling down - we all fall down when we're learning to walk. The day comes when the little toddler stands up for the first time, pulling herself up, with the help from some nearby furniture, to a standing position. She wobbles about for a few seconds and then falls down. Not to be deterred, she gets up by herself and tries again, determined to take some steps. As a loving parent you watch on attentively, offering assistance to buffer the next fall. Yet you know and fully understand that your little toddler must learn to walk on her own. For days this goes on and eventually the toddler is able to string together a few steps, but then falls down again. You, as a loving parent, continue to watch on patiently, offering encouraging words, because you know that your little toddler is improving every day and soon she'll be walking without any of your assistance. You might even get a little chuckle when she takes an awkward fall. As a loving parent you understand that it's perfectly normal for your little toddler to fall down. You would never take your little toddler aside and scold her or punish her for falling down because you know that the falling down is a part of learning to walk. Besides, as a loving parent, you know that scolding and punishing will not make a difference. In fact, it would make the situation worse. Instead, you wait patiently.

You help her up, brush her off, comfort her, and lead her on her way again. In other words, the "falling down" is perfect development for your little toddler as she grows and learns to walk. In learning to walk, your little toddler is absolutely perfect! Well, this is how God is looking at us, as we make this incredible journey from being good Gods to great Gods. The life we are leading today looks imperfect from earthly terms, but from a spiritual perspective we are developing perfectly[84]. All of our NDErs, covered here, came back with the message that everyone's life is of great importance. The testimonies from the documented accounts tell us that each and every life is an essential part of a bigger picture, a larger plan.

> *"You can make an empty shell, but you cannot express nothing at all. You can wait, delay, paralyze yourself, or reduce your creativity almost to nothing. But you cannot abolish it. You can destroy your medium of communication, but not your potential. You did not create yourself."*[85]

God-through-Helen (ACIM, T-1.V.1:4-8)

Through this life lived, we are constantly learning and growing as spiritual beings. Each of us is a student, and each of us is a teacher pursuing our own spiritual growth and helping others to achieve their own spiritual growth. Through our lives lived, we experience and learn through our challenges, struggles, and suffering. There are life lessons and experiences in compassion, empathy, unconditional love of self, unconditional love for others, patience, forgiveness, communication, gratitude, courage, kindness, tolerance, respectfulness, power, independence, perseverance, loss, faith, humility, and many, many others - all of them wonderful aspects of godliness that we are here to experience and master.

Like "the diamond in the rough", we are being reshaped, refined, and polished to an extraordinary clarity and brilliance. Our very existence here on earth means that you and I are striving, making every effort to expand our spirit and raise our consciousness to fully develop into the truly magnificent Gods that we are meant to be.

Chapter 9

WE ARE ALL ONE

"The parts of Me that have become the
lot of You are what We are talking about
here. Thus, the Divine Dichotomy:
There is only One of us. There are Many of us."

GOD-THROUGH-NEALE, CONVERSATIONS WITH GOD: BOOK 3

In *Conversations with God* brought through Neale and the "Course in Miracles" brought through Helen, God continually emphasizes a key point: We are all one - we are all part of the one great spirit of God. That is to say that we are a part of the body of God - not poetically or philosophically but literally a part of the body of God. After all, where do you think our divine, spiritual magnificence came from? This is not to say that we descended from God in the beginning and have since become separate and distinct from God, as many of our religions teach. We continue to be a part of God and God continues to be a part of us. When we are lumbering around in a physical body, feeling physically separate from God and each other, the illusion of separation is very powerful. We believe that we are separate bodies; in separate families; of separate races, cultures, and religions; and in separated cities and separate countries. Our idea of separation affects all aspects of life on our planet. Throughout our human history, the idea of separation or this "consciousness of separation" is behind all of our warring, killing, suffering, and fighting with one another.[86] It is an illusion nonetheless - we are never ever alone or separate from God.

> "You are, have always been, and will always be, a divine part of the divine whole, a member of the body. That is why the act of rejoining the whole, of returning to God, is called remembrance. You actually choose to re-member Who You Really Are, or to join together with the various parts of you to experience the all of you - which is to say, the All of Me."[87]

> God-through-Neale

All of the NDErs who have been discussed earlier reported that during their NDE, they experienced feelings of oneness with all things in the universe. In God's conversation with Neale, God explains the illusion of separation using a brilliant and original analogy. God goes on to tell Neale, "It's like the air in your house." There is really only one very large body of air around the planet and circulating through, in, and around everything - including your home. You may walk into your kitchen and smell dinner cooking. If you walk over into the family room, you smell the fire burning in the fireplace. It seems that there is a separate air in the kitchen and a separate air in the family room, but there's no one place where the air in the kitchen ends and the air in the family room begins. Yet the air in the kitchen still seems separate and distinct from the air in the living room - because it smells different. You may go into another room where the air seems stale and open a window to let in some fresh air, but that too is from the same large body of air. There is only one large body of air moving in, through, and around all the rooms in the house, even though it can seem like separate air. In the kitchen you smell dinner, and in the family room you smell the fire burning in the fireplace. There is no separate air; there is only one body of air that seems different in different localities of the house. That is to say that the air in the various parts of the house exhibits different attributes. Yet all the air belongs to the same large body of air that envelops the planet. Living as unique, spiritual beings in separate physical bodies, it seems and it appears that we are separate from God and each other, but we are really extensions of the same magnificent, divine spirit. This is the "divine dichotomy": There is only one great spirit, but there are many spirits making up the one great spirit.[88]

"I was mistaken when I thought I lived apart from God, a separate entity that moved in isolation, unattached, and housed within a body. Now I know my life is God's, I have no other home, and I do not exist apart from Him."[89]

God-Through-Helen (ACIM, W-PII.223.1:1-2)

FORGETTING WHO WE REALLY ARE

How can one feel so alone and isolated, at times, when we're supposed to be "one with God"? We all know what it's like to feel alone. Oftentimes it can feel like it's you against a big cruel world - that's understandable. In *Conversations with God*, God describes this dilemma, explaining that we must first forget who we are and where it is we come from so that we can use this lifetime to recreate a new, grander version of ourselves. I know that this can sound very confusing, but there is method to the apparent madness.

> "As I have described now several times, this forgetting is 'built into the system.'
>
> It is part of the process. For you cannot create Who You Are until you forget Who You Are.
>
> So the illusion causing forgetfulness is an effect created on purpose."[90]

> *God-through-Neale*

Roy Mills is a man with a very unique gift. Unlike you and me, Roy has been permitted to keep his memories of his pre-birth life in heaven and the purpose of his current life. Thus, Roy is able to fully recall the memory of his own spiritual magnificence and his heavenly home. His life story and pre-birth recollections are documented in his book *A Soul's Remembrance: Earth is Not Our Home*. Roy's very insightful life story supports the ancient idea of "pre-existence of the soul." Each life is an opportunity to recreate ourselves anew. With the spiritual growth that we receive from a lifetime, we are transformed into a wiser, more enhanced version of ourselves, progressing ever closer to our godly magnificence. This forgetfulness that is sometimes referred to as "being on the other side of the veil" is necessary in order for us to have our earthly experiences. Roy explains this essential need for "forgetfulness" in more detail:

> *"Before long most children forget that they are mighty spirit beings who came from Heaven. That forgetfulness is part of God's plan, because if we could keep talking to angels and remembering Heaven every waking moment, we would limit the earthly experiences we are meant to have by constantly choosing what is right. And so much of what we must learn and experience comes from making the wrong choice and suffering because of it."[91]*

God did not make a mistake. Although we cannot always remember or feel our close connection to God, we are eternally "joined at the hip", so to speak. Whether we like it or not, our union with God is permanent and complete. We couldn't separate ourselves from God even if we tried. It would be like a light bulb saying, "I want to continue to shine brightly, completely independent of everything", then abruptly pulling the plug from its one and only power source. Without the power source, there can be no light. Upon our completion of this lifetime and our return to the spiritual realm, not only will we know the deep peace and tranquility of heaven, but we will experience the blissful reunion with God.

> *"You'll look back at the first stage and call it purgatory. The second stage, when you can have anything you want with the speed of*

*your thought, you'll call heaven. The third stage, when you experi-
ence the bliss of the Oneness, you'll call nirvana."*[92]

God-through-Neale

Every day we bear witness to such insane acts of violence, sense-
less shooting and killing, and the atrocious suffering in war-torn
countries. This brings us to the next question: Why does evil exist
at all? After all, if God has unconditional love for us and we are
truly extensions of God's great spirit, then why do we see so much
evil in the world today?

THE PURPOSE OF EVIL

God's greatest gift to us is "free will" - a free will to be whoever we
choose to be in this lifetime. Free will isn't really "free"; it comes
with a price: the freedom to make good choices and decisions that
work to our advantage and the freedom to make bad choices and
decisions that work to our disadvantage. In Eben's NDE and subsequent communion with God, as well as Neale's communion with
God, God confirms that a small amount of evil is necessary in the
physical realm so that we may have full freedom to exercise our
free will and know ourselves as we truly are.[93]

In this way, you and I have a wide ranging field of experience and
an unrestricted opportunity to better know and understand ourselves
through our actions, decisions, and choices. If we make a bad decision
or a wrong choice, then we endure the consequences and even have
the freedom to continue with the bad choices and decisions for as long
as it suits us. God is not going to choose for us or decide for us.

To give an example, let's say that you've been raised all your life on a steady diet of fresh fruits and cereal - you've never eaten anything else. Given these circumstances, you really wouldn't have any idea of all the foods that you'd like or dislike to eat - you wouldn't know your diet. Then one day you are introduced to a bountiful buffet that features all the delicious foods you've never tasted before. There are delectable dishes of chicken, seafood, beef, rice, BBQ, vegetables, salads, pasta, sushi, soups, and a sweet table filled with all the desserts and pastries you can possibly imagine - tables and tables of delicious goodness. The buffet is all free and available to you every day for two weeks. After eating at the buffet for a number of days, you begin to get a sense of what you like and what you don't like at the buffet. Perhaps you come to know yourself as a vegetarian, or a meat and potatoes type, or someone who likes a little bit of everything. Given the opportunity to taste and sample many different foods, you now know more about yourself - for one thing, you know more about your diet. In similar fashion, God gives us a lifetime to taste and sample from a vast selection of experiences including the experience called "evil". In making our decisions and choices, we decide and declare who we are - a process of self-discovery whereby we use our own free will to come to know ourselves more fully.

> "I do not show My goodness by creating only what you call perfection all around you.
>
> I do not demonstrate My love by not allowing you to demonstrate yours."[94]
>
> God-through-Neale

Existence of evil in our world also creates a context whereby we can know and experience the opposite of evil, such as love and compassion. In God's wisdom, we come to recognize that nothing can exist in our world without its opposite. We cannot experience hot, if there is no cold. We cannot experience fast, unless there is slow. We cannot know up, unless there is down; and we cannot experience love, unless there is evil.[95] This can be difficult to accept, but at this stage of our spiritual development, the evil serves its purpose. It serves as a stepping stone to take us to a higher level of consciousness and a new improved version of ourselves. As we walk this incredible journey from being good Gods to great Gods, we encounter opportunities to experience evil. Some of us will avoid the experience altogether, while others may choose to sample it and some of us will fully indulge ourselves in this experience until we simply grow tired and eventually put it aside and move on. Mr. James Guilliani is a shining example of someone who has made this transition in his lifetime. His experience is documented in his true life story called *Dogfella: How An Abandoned Dog Named Bruno Turned This Mobster's Life Around.*

While working as a cold-hearted mob enforcer for some of New York's biggest organized crime families, he one day rescues a severely abused and abandoned Shih Tzu dog that had been chained to a parking meter and left for dead. The state of the poor dog evokes compassion in James and he adopts the little dog and makes every attempt to nurse it back to health. James tells the inspiring story about his journey from the life of mob enforcer to a caring, kind, and compassionate human being who now runs a successful dog grooming business and provides a shelter for homeless animals. Somehow this little homeless dog manages to inspire James, melt his hardened heart, and transform him forever[96]. When I hear James's story, I can't help but think of our own dog "Bella", a six-year-old Wheaton Terrier that provides us with laughter and is constantly enriching our lives with her abundant unconditional love, attention, and companionship. One man who has had dogs around him all his life remarked that a dog was one of God's greatest creations. On further reflection, he said that originally he thought that we were here to take care of them, but as he looks back on his own life, he now believes that they are here to take care of us. It's no coincidence that "d-o-g", spelled backwards, is "god".

In the spiritual transformation of James Guilliani, James's life is the perfect example of how we develop spiritually.

This is how God's teaching is so different from our own traditional institutions of learning. The lessons are not hammered into us from the outside-in, but rather they arise from our own personal experience. This way, the lesson emerges internally from the inside-out. God's method is much more effective because the lesson is coming from you rather than at you.[97]

"You can temporize and you are capable of enormous procrastination, but you cannot depart entirely from your creator, who set the limits on your ability to mis-create. An imprisoned will engenders a situation which, in the extreme, becomes altogether intolerable. Tolerance for pain may be high, but it is not without limit. Eventually everyone begins to recognize, however dimly, that there must be a better way."[98]

God-through-Helen (ACIM, T-2.III.3.1:3-6)

It's my belief that one way or another we all must pass through and grow our spirit beyond the need to experience evil. I'm not saying that we have to like evil or condone it. There are many things that benefit us that we don't always like, such as working out, cod liver oil, or a root canal. I'm only saying that the existence of evil is there for our spiritual growth to ultimately make us better, like the spiritual transformation of Mr. James Guillani. If it hasn't already happened, there will be a day in our own spiritual journey when we no longer have the need to experience evil. We see so much evil in our world today because, as individuals and a society, we are freely choosing evil and deciding to experience evil - it's that simple. We could easily decide to make a new choice or a different choice, but we haven't done that.

"Trials are but lessons that you failed to learn presented once again, so where you made a faulty choice before you now can make a better one, and thus escape all pain that what you chose before has brought to you. In every difficulty, all distress, and each perplexity God calls to you and gently says, 'My brother/sister, choose again.'"[99]

God-through-Helen (ACIM, T-31.VII.3:1-2)

THERE IS NO HELL...SORRY

For me, a God of unlimited and unconditional love destroys any idea of a Hell or eternal damnation. After all, if you're going to spend an eternity in Hell, there has to be a God to disown you, put you there, and prevent you from entering Heaven...right? The idea of a Hell or an organized dark force ruled by a Satan figure makes for good television shows, movies, video games, fiction novels, and religious rant, but my life experience hasn't shown me that. In the course of my research, I haven't come across any examples of desperate spirits trapped forever in the eternal fires of Hell. Since I know now that God loves unconditionally and the spirit of God lives in each of us, I simply can't believe in a devil or the existence of Hell. Just like the archaic belief that God can somehow be hurt, damaged, or offended, or that God needs and demands our perfection, these are nothing more than the unfounded imaginings of men. Hell and eternal damnation are nothing more than fear tactics, still used today and for thousands of years, by our fear-based religions to attract and retain their memberships.

> "Yet the good news is that there is no reason for fear, no cause to be scared. No one is going to judge you, no one is going to make you "wrong," no one is going to throw you into the everlasting fires of hell." "Each of you has constructed, within the framework of your own particular theology, some idea, some concept of God's Worst Punishment. And I hate to tell you this, because I see the fun you're having with the drama of it all, but, well,...just ain't no such thing."[100]

> God-Through-Neale

When we hear of terrible crime, gross injustice, or outright wrongdoing, it's completely natural for human beings to feel upset, angry, and indignant. We want the person or persons responsible to be punished, to suffer, and to be held accountable for their actions. We desire vengeance and payback so much so that we can even judge ourselves harshly when we believe that we've committed a wrongdoing. We're capable of carrying around guilt and shame for decades at a time, refusing to forgive ourselves. Since we are so unforgiving, we believe that God is unforgiving too. It becomes almost impossible for us to imagine a God that rises above all of that.[101] At one point in Neale's conversation with God, Neale is ready to walk away and abandon the task of scribing his conversation with God. Can you imagine telling God that you no longer want to write down Her words? He cites the fact that his own life has been far from perfect. He acknowledges his many mistakes and the hurt he's caused to his family and his own children. Neale goes on in total, self-deprecating fashion, telling God that he is unworthy - so unworthy. For these reasons, Neale sincerely requests that God release him from his writing duties. God responds to Neale's request as only a God of unconditional love and compassion can respond. I include God's response to Neale here because I know that this is a message that is meant for all of us to hear:

> "Yet I tell you this. You are worthy. As is everyone else. Unworthiness is the worst indictment ever visited upon the human race. You have based your sense of worthiness on the past, while I base your sense of worthiness on the future.
>
> The future, the future always the future!
>
> That is where your life is, not in the past.
>
> The future. That is where truth is, not in the past.
>
> What you have done is unimportant compared to what you are about to do.
>
> How you have erred is insignificant compared to how you are about to create.
>
> I forgive your mistakes. All of them.
>
> I forgive your misplaced passions. All of them.
>
> I forgive your erroneous notions, your misguided understandings, your hurtful actions, your selfish decisions. All of them.

Others may not forgive you, but I do.

Others will not release you from your guilt, but I do.

Others may not let you forget, allow you to go on, become something new, but I do.

For I know that you are not what you were, but are and always will be, what you are now."[102]

God-through-Neale

It only gets better! Not only do we see a God with unconditional love and compassion, but this exemplifies God's unfathomable capacity for forgiveness and mercy.

As promised, I would like to use the next three chapters to show how science is moving towards the same conclusions as spirituality. You may find these next chapters interesting to better understand how modern science is supporting spirituality. That is to say, scientific advancements over the past three decades are finding evidence of the God in you and the God in the universe.

Chapter 10

FINALLY...SCIENCE FINDS THE GOD IN YOU

"Our progeny will shake their heads with disbelief over the arrogance we displayed in our meager understanding of nature. It took three hundred years of hard-won scientific advances merely to verify the existence of something that people had been experiencing for millennia."

DEAN RADIN, PhD - *THE CONSCIOUS UNIVERSE*

For centuries, science and religion have held opposing philosophical views about God and life. This dualism seems destined to go on for eternity in an ever-widening chasm between viewpoints and beliefs. Some might be surprised to know that science and religion have not always been in a state of discord. There was a time in our brief history when science and religion were in perfect harmony holding complementary views of God and life. Both sides were in full agreement and steadfast in the notion that humankind and our planet were at the center of the entire universe. Our position at the center of the universe was explicitly stated in holy scriptures and the early church had already built up whole theologies around this doctrine. The sun, the stars, and all the other celestial bodies, as wondrous as they were, all revolved around us. Unfortunately, like all good relationships, the honeymoon between science and religion was not to last forever. The first cracks in the foundation began when a young mathematician and astronomer named Nicolaus Copernicus (1473 - 1543), who was charting the movement of the stars, revealed his findings to the church, thereby showing that our Earth was not at the center of the universe at all. The sun and the stars were not revolving around us, but rather it was our planet that was revolving around the sun. Despite the evidence that Copernicus was presenting, the early church stood in staunch denial of any such notion. Copernicus was labeled a heretic and forced to recant his findings. Decades later, the famous astronomer, physicist, engineer, and mathematician Galileo Galilei (1564 - 1642) came along and told the early church that he had definitive proof that Copernicus was right and we were not at the center of the universe. The early church labeled Galileo a heretic and blasphemer and he too, to say the least, was forced to recant his findings.[103] The conflict between the scientific worldview and the religious worldview was now beginning to unfold. Science went on to show that we were not even at the center of the galaxy, let alone the universe. The universe itself had no center, but was actually infinite and eternal. Gradually, more and more, science was chipping away at our prominence and grandeur in the universe. It seemed that science would eventually provide all the answers to life's greatest mysteries. It was thought that religion and spirituality would have to take a back seat while science was taking us steadily down the road to scientific enlightenment. With the advancements in technology and accumulated scientific knowledge, it was only a matter of time before science could provide all the evidence needed to support the classical, scientific view that human beings, our world and our universe, worked very much like machines. Science was showing us that virtually everything - from the movement of planetary bodies, down to the inner factory-like workings in a single human cell - could be accurately measured, meticulously calculated, and neatly categorized. By the nineteenth century, the scientific community had painted a purely materialistic picture of the world, where all the necessary, purposeful events taking place in the universe were just as sure and predictable as clockwork. Through the eyes of the classical, scientific view of the universe, you and I have been left out, demoted - reduced in size and stature to nothing more than little, inconsequential parts of a larger machine.[104] However, just as we were beginning to believe in our own insignificance and "littleness" in the world, the tables have begun to turn. The classical scientific model that up until now had overlooked our position in the universe is being dismantled and demolished for the rebuilding of a new scientific model of physical reality. This is a model that recognizes our godliness and positions us back in our rightful place as an indispensable element in the universe. Thanks to advanced technology and the hard work of many brilliant scientists, the scientific viewpoint has come around full circle. The same advances in technology that once diminished any prospect of our own godliness now serve to prove and reinforce the evidence of the God that resides in each of us.

We also have to recognize that all of these frontier explorers - scientists, medical doctors, and researchers - are all great risk-takers. In pursuing these unchartered fields of study, they sacrifice it all - research funding, career and reputation. They should all be acknowledged for their initiative, courage, and dedication in presenting their new ideas and theories. Don't get me wrong; new ideas and theories are accepted, but when they challenge long held scientific doctrines and beliefs, they are met with resistance. Even when coming from brilliant scientists from very good schools with very good credentials and impeccable scientific work records, presenting these new ideas and theories can still be an extremely difficult task.

One area of study that has been persistently ignored and maligned by mainstream science is the unending human experience of extrasensory perception or ESP. Premonitions, personal intuition, self-healing, dream revelation, and the power of prayer happen every day in the human experience, but have been largely ignored by mainstream science because they do not fit the current scientific model of how the world is presumed to work. All that changed nearly three decades ago when a group of dedicated scientists astounded the scientific community. In 1989, physicist Robert G. Jahn and clinical psychologist Brenda J. Dunne, both at Princeton University, announced that after a decade of rigorous experimentation by their Princeton Engineering Anomalies Research Laboratory (PEAR), they had accumulated unequivocal evidence that the mind can psychically interact with physical reality. This was astounding, because nowhere in the current scientific model of physical reality did mainstream science account for the ability of human beings to psychically interact with physical reality.[105]

One of the members of this research team was Dean Radin, PhD, a senior scientist at the institute of Noetic Sciences (ION) and founder of the Consciousness Research Laboratory at the University of Nevada, Las Vegas. He held appointments at Princeton University, the University of Edinburgh, and several Silicon Valley think tanks and produced cutting-edge parapsychological research for AT&T, Contel, SRI International, and the U.S. government. Radin has been described as "The Einstein of Parapsychology" for his vast experience, dedication, and exceptional work in the research and study of extra sensory perception (ESP) or psychic ability in human beings. In scientific circles, the study of human psychic ability is simply referred to as "psi" (pronounced sigh). Over the decades Radin has witnessed the introduction and acceptance of new innovative theories into the scientific community. He claims that there are four stages that every new theory must pass through. In stage one, the skeptics claim that the idea is impossible because it violates the laws of science. In the second stage the skeptics reluctantly concede that the idea is possible but not very interesting and the effects are extremely weak. In the third stage the mainstream realizes that the idea is important and the effects have a greater impact than previously thought. Finally, in the fourth stage the same critics that had first dismissed the idea now claim that they thought of it first.[106]

It would be misleading to portray Dr. Dean Radin as the only one leading the charge on psi research. Like many great scientific revelations, Radin's work has been based on the work of other dedicated scientists working before him and alongside him who produced documented research on psi. Radin outlines the history, current state, and applications of psi research in his book entitled *The Conscious Universe: The Scientific Truth of Psychic Phenomena.* Radin explains that the ongoing research into psi focuses on two areas. The first area involves the ability to perceive objects and events beyond the range of ordinary senses, and the second area involves the ability to mentally cause action at a distance.[107]

CAUSING ACTION AT A DISTANCE

One of the first automated instruments that scientists used to measure psi was a "random number generator" or RNG. As the technology was refined, scientist called the machine a "random event generator" or REG machine. Both machines used complex methodologies to generate random numbers. These machines worked like giant coin-flippers, randomly selecting a string of numbers that could either be a one for heads or a zero for tails (i.e. 00110110…). When left alone to operate without interference and simply left to chance, the REG would typically generate a result of approximately fifty percent heads and fifty percent tails - just as you'd expect. This is exactly how the REG machine was designed to operate. The next step was for scientists to measure the impact of psi. To do this they would recruit a number of subjects and re-quest that they attempt to alter the outcome of the REG machine by focusing their intention on creating more heads than tails or vice-versa. If the outcome of the REG machine deviated from the normal fifty-fifty pattern resulting from chance alone, then scientist would assume that the intention of the subjects was affecting the REG machine.[108]

In analyzing the results of the REG machine experiments, Radin, Jahn, and Dunne did not restrict their research to just their own experiments, but embarked on a statistical grind that looked at the combined REG machine experiments conducted over decades from different research scientists on different populations in different laboratories around the world - a practice known as meta-analysis. In this way, you're not looking at the results of a group of individuals. Instead, the meta-analysis allows scientists to see how people perform in general, across many experiments. This provides a much more rich and comprehensive picture of the results of psi research. What they found in the compiled results was nothing short of astonishing. Without a doubt, the meta-analysis showed convincingly that ordinary human beings like you and me were able to influence the outcome of the REG machines through our focused intention.[109] According to conventional science, we're not supposed to be able to affect an object from a distance, but the resulting data from thousands of REG machine experiments on thousands of subjects show that human beings possess this unique ability.

REMOTE VIEWING

Another area of psi research that is backed by more than six decades of experimentation is the practice of remote viewing. Remote viewing is the ability of normal, everyday people to telepathically perceive the images observed by another person who is stationed in a remote location. For best results, the person that will receive the images is placed into a relaxed state, removing all possible distractions and limiting sensory input. To give an example, I could be standing in front of the CN tower in Toronto, Canada focusing my thoughts on the scene before me and mentally projecting these images. In turn, you could be quietly relaxing in a hot tub at Whistler Mountain in British Columbia. In a relaxed state, with minimal sensory input and no distraction, you would begin to telepathically see the images that I am projecting in your mind's eye. There is nothing new here. Radin points out that there are ancient yoga texts from India, such as Patanjali's Yoga Sutras that date back thirty-five hundred years. These ancient texts tell us that we are able to reach higher states of consciousness and experience various psychic abilities through prolonged deep meditation. Similar effects occur naturally during dreaming, prior to falling asleep, under hypnosis, with some drugs, and in sensory isolation chambers. The essential requirement for remote viewing is to remove sensory distractions and quiet the mind.[110]

If the thought had crossed your mind that remote viewing could be useful strategically for military purposes, you're absolutely right. This is how remote viewing was brought to the forefront of psi research and gained the attention of government and military. Radin states that World War II historians have documented the use of remote viewing during the war. Secret British Army documents revealed that the head of Britain's Royal Air Force, the man credited with winning the "Battle of Britain", had a wife that was a "sensitive". She was adept at remote viewing and was credited with using remote viewing to locate enemy air bases that conventional methods had not detected.[111]

Former Los Angeles police commissioner the late Pat Price was a gifted psychic who assisted psi researchers in psychic experimentation and in the refinement of remote viewing techniques. Working for the Los Angeles police department, Price had used his psychic abilities to capture criminals cold in their tracks. Price would sit inside the dispatch room and wait for the crime to be reported. Once the call was received, Price would scan the city mentally and settle on a time and place where he visualized the suspect would be. Price claimed that he invariably caught the criminal just where he visualized that person would be. Through research and experimentation, Price showed scientists that remote viewing was not at all affected by distance, deep water obstructions, or even specially shielded enclosures. Price was a gifted psychic, so he was the perfect subject for researching. Yet the research showed that most of the general public possess the ability to do remote viewing.[112]

In the 1950s at the height of the Cold War, both the American and Russian governments funded psi research. There were secret CIA-funded programs involving some psi research that were code named "Bluebird" and "Artichoke". Beginning in the Cold War years, the psi research was highly classified for two reasons. First of all, governments realized that psi, especially remote viewing, could provide an advantage in strategic military intelligence work. Secondly, the research was politically and scientifically controversial. Government agencies knew that they would be exposed to the same ridicule that led academic and industrial scientists to be discreet in publicizing their interest in psi. It was only in 1995 when the information became declassified and the rumors of secret government funding into psi research could be confirmed by the scientists and other personnel that were involved. To get some idea about the critical importance of remote viewing, the bulk of the U.S. government-supported funding on psi research involved remote viewing.[113] Dean Radin was one of those scientists, on the inside looking out, when remote viewing was being intensely researched by the U.S. government and the military. In summary of the research, Radin provides these insights:

"Scientists who had worked on these highly classified programs, including myself, were frustrated to know firsthand the reality of high-performance psi phenomena and yet we had no way of publicly responding to skeptics. Nothing could be said about the fact that the U.S. Army had supported a secret team of remote viewers, that those viewers had participated in hundreds of remote-viewing missions, and that the DIA, CIA, Customs Service, Drug Enforcement Administration, FBI, and Secret Service had all relied on the remote-viewing team for more than a decade, sometimes with startling results. Now, finally, the history of American and Soviet military and intelligence-sponsored psi research is emerging as participants come forward to document their experiences."[114]

THE FEELING OF BEING STARED AT

You're standing in the supermarket check-out line, patiently waiting for the next available cashier. You begin to get an odd feeling, nothing that you could put your finger on, but it can only be described as a very subtle uneasiness. Whatever it is, it seems to be coming from behind you. You turn around to find a person staring at you directly. At first you wonder who this stranger could be, and then you recognize that it's your former co-worker. Yes, why it's Jasmine - who used to work in the office with you several months ago! You smile and give her a slightly awkward wave.

What you've just experienced is the feeling of being stared at. This is an everyday common experience that we've all had. Radin reveals that "the feeling of being stared at" has been studied in the lab for over a century. Lab tests have evolved to the point where the two people (the person being stared at - the "staree" and the person doing the staring - the "starer") are not even located in the same room. All the staring is done via close circuit camera to eliminate any chance of sensory input. In one room the staree is hooked-up to a number of sensors that monitor the staree's physiology. Since the staring is done via close circuit camera, the staree doesn't have any idea exactly when they are being stared at. Test results show that the staree's nervous system is subtly affected when they are being stared at, and in most cases the staree is not even aware that there has been any change in their physiology. This suggests that the act of people looking at us affects us more than we know. This, like the REG machines, demonstrates that human beings possess the ability to cause action at a distance by subtly affecting the nervous system in another person located some distance away.[115]

DISTANCE HEALING THROUGH PRAYER

In 1996 two scientists named Dr. Elisabeth Targ and Dr. Fred Sicher embarked on the challenging task of determining if they could find scientific evidence for the healing power of prayer. Targ was a psychiatrist and the daughter of Dr. Russel Targ, a scientist who had been involved in remote viewing experiments at SRI International. Sicher was a retired psychologist and researcher. At the time, Targ was living in San Francisco at the height of the AIDS epidemic. After witnessing firsthand the devastating human toll of the AIDS virus, Targ was skeptical about the possibility of any effective healing through prayer. It was her father's previous success with remote viewing experiments at SRI International that gave her any hope. The evidence from remote viewing was encouraging to her because it strongly argued for the existence of some sort of extrasensory connection between people and a field that connected all things.[116]

Together, Targ and Sicher worked for months to prepare a stringent protocol for conducting the clinical trial, taking every precaution to ensure that any healing would be due only to the healing effects of prayer. The experiment consisted of forty male patients suffering from advanced stage AIDS virus, divided into two groups: one group that would not be treated with prayer (the control group) and a second group that would be treated with prayer (treatment group). They selected patients with similar attributes: having end stage AIDS, being of the same age, having the same T-cell count, the same degree of illnesses, the same prescribed medications, and so on. Next, Targ and Sicher went out and selected the healers who would pray for the treatment group of AIDS patients. The protocol designed for the healers was just as rigorous. Targ and Sicher immediately excluded healers who appeared to be overly egotistical and/or fraudulent; furthermore, the healers had to be dedicated because they would receive neither money nor personal glory for their efforts. Targ and Sicher gathered forty healers in all from diverse cultures, backgrounds, and healing methods. Of the forty healers, some were religious, while others were spiritual. There were Christian healers, a Jewish Kabbalist, some Buddhists, and others from non-denominational healing schools such as the Barbara Brennan School of Healing Light. Still other healers worked with ancient techniques. A Qigong master from China would send qi energy to patients, and an American Lakota Sioux shaman would rely on an age-old Native American pipe smoking ceremony. Finally, all the healers would have to show that they had had previous success with the distant healing of critically-ill patients. The frequency and duration of the healing prayer was also strictly regimented. Each healer would pray one hour a day, six days a week for ten weeks, with alternate weeks off for rest. To eliminate any bias, every patient in the treatment group would be prayed for by a different healer each week. These healers never met the patients in person, but would only receive envelopes containing the patient's name, picture, and some health-related details.[117]

In some scientific experiments the patients would be randomly assigned so that they wouldn't know if they were part of the treatment group or not. Only the attending physicians would know which patients made up the treatment group. This is known as a "single-blind" experiment. In another type of experiment, the patients wouldn't know if they were in the treatment group and the attending physicians wouldn't know which patients were in the treatment group either. This second type of experiment is known as a "double-blind" experiment and is used to eliminate any chance that a patient may receive special attention or favoritism from the attending physician. For this experiment, Targ and Sicher selected to use a double-blind experiment.

Targ couldn't believe the results that she was looking at. The members of the treatment group were undeniably healthier on all fronts with fewer doctor visits, fewer hospitalizations, fewer days in hospital, and significantly lower severity of the disease! For Targ and Sicher the evidence was irrevocable. No matter what healing method was used or what belief was held in a higher being, the healers had demonstrated that distant healing with prayer is very effective. Through consistent prayer or what Targ called "focused intention for the well-being of another", the AIDS patients had responded miraculously to the treatment!

One may look at the final results of these experiments in distant healing as conclusive evidence that God exists, or at least answers prayers and heals the sick. But this is not the conclusion that scientists have drawn from these studies. Not all the healers in these experiments called on God, Jesus, or other religious figures for their healing. Scientists point out that the one common factor across all methods of distant healing was the ability to focus an intention for the health and well-being of the patient.[118] Now science has the evidence, but it's no secret that religion and spirituality have been using the benefits of prayer for thousands of years - not only to heal the sick, but also to improve all aspects of people's lives.

"The soul remembers in the next life what it would have been well to remember in this life-that all effect is created by thought, and that manifestation is a result of intention."[119]

God-through-Neale

SEEING INTO THE FUTURE

A premonition is the perception, through feelings, visions, or dreams of an event or situation that will take place in the future. For those of us who are in touch with our intuition, this happens quite frequently, but for others, experiencing a premonition may only occur when there is a life-changing event or situation at hand. The premonition may be the foretelling of something good that is about to happen or the forewarning of something unfortunate that is about to happen in our lives. Some of us will call this innate intuition a "hunch" or a "gut-feeling", but it's all referring to the same thing.

Human beings have a natural reflex action to certain physical stimuli. For example, if an object quickly passes near to your eye, we naturally blink. If the doctor taps your knee in just the precise spot, your leg will automatically kick forward. We are not just limited to physical reflex actions; we also have reflex actions that involve the mind and the body. Reflex actions that engage the mind and body are called "psychophysical reflexes". One common example of the psychophysical reflex is called the "orienting response" or the "fight or flight response". This natural reflex is more pronounced when we or our loved ones face a situation of imminent danger, but the reflex is also invoked in a less threatening context like facing an entirely new stimuli or situation - such as a request for an impromptu speech at your friend's wedding. The orienting response is made manifest by physical changes in the body, such as dilation of the pupils, altered brain-waves, a rise in sweat-gland activity, or a rise/fall pattern in the heart-rate and blanching of the extremities, just to name a few. These bodily changes serve to support our survival by enhancing us with improved decision making, increased strength, and a reduced danger of bleeding. Today we have technology that can accurately read and measure these bodily indicators, which makes them ideal for study in a lab environment.[120]

While at the University of Nevada, Las Vegas, Radin and others conducted experiments to determine if the human nervous system would react to future events before they happen. To conduct this experiment they used photographs displayed on a computer monitor. There were two groups of photographs. One group of pictures featured beautiful landscapes, cheerful people, and scenes of nature. These photographs were considered the "calm" photographs because they tended to invoke a calm response from the viewer.

The other group of pictures were the "emotional pictures", and as you may have guessed, they depicted disturbing and shocking scenes that invoked an emotional response from the viewer. The experiment was designed so that the computer would randomly select and display a vivid, high definition picture from a pool of 120 photos with a short five-second interval between photos. The viewer would sit in front of the monitor and view the random photos, all the while being monitored to measure their orienting response. Radin and team then charted the activity of the orienting response before, during, and after viewing the photographs. The results of the experiment showed that the viewers' orienting response was active just before they viewed photographs, but their orienting response was most active before they viewed the emotional photos. The most significant findings from these experiments is that ordinary human beings "pre-act" to their own future emotional state, what's known as "presentiment". The other interesting note from these experiments is that the participants were not consciously aware that they had a physical reaction to the emotional photographs, indicating that presentiment is largely an unconscious process.[121] Countless survivors and victims had chilling premonitions of September 9/11. Some heeded those premonitions and others ignored them. There are nineteen documented cases of people who had premonitions about the sinking of the Titanic. Some passengers paid attention to the premonition and survived, other passengers ignored their premonition and drowned, and some were not in either of those two groups.[122] The evidence of presentiment and premonitions demonstrates the human ability to perceive objects and events beyond the range of ordinary senses. Currently, continuing research into psi is no longer asking the question: "Does psi exist?" The focus has now shifted to questions like "How does it work?" and "What influences psi performance?"[123]

"You all have what you call "psychic power." It is, truly, a sixth sense. And you all have a "sixth sense about things." Psychic power is simply the ability to step out of your limited experience into a broader view. To step back. To feel more than what the limited individual you have imagined yourself to be would feel; to know more than he or she would know. It is the ability to tap into the larger truth all around you; to sense a different energy."[124]

God-Through-Neale

First there were centuries of fear, persecution, and witch hunts against anyone who claimed to have any psychic abilities. In more modern times we've gained a modicum of tolerance, but we still resided in doubt, skepticism, and denial at any notion that psi could be for real. Finally, we are slowly beginning to move to acceptance. As one of the pioneers who has spent decades on the frontlines of psi research, Radin had this to say, as he looks back and reflects upon the uphill struggle to finally prove scientifically the existence of psi:

"So far, we've learned that the effects observed in a thousand psi experiments are not due to chance, selective reporting, variations in experimental quality, or design flaws. They've been independently replicated by competent, conventionally trained scientists at well-known academic, industrial, and government-supported laboratories worldwide for more than a century, and the effects are consistent with human experiences reported throughout history and across all cultures. We've also learned that one of the main reasons this evidence is largely unknown is that psi effects do not fit the preconceptions underlying conventional scientific theories."[125]

The other imperative fact identified in the centuries of psi research is that all of us have these abilities. It is a natural part of our spiritual make-up. Now, that's not to say that we all use our psychic power, but the opportunity is always there to develop our psi faculties more fully. Like muscles, we all have them, but some of us will develop them and some of us won't. Some of us have an extraordinary sense of taste. Some of us have extraordinary eyesight. Some of us have exquisite hearing with the ability to pick out that one slightly off-key note in a Mozart piano concerto. Some of us have special talents in music, art, athleticism, or mathematics, and some of us have remarkable psychic ability. Similarly, we can all paint a picture but we can't all paint a picture worthy of hanging in the national art gallery. We readily accept the fact that people possess special talents, but we're more skeptical when applying this to individual psychic ability.

Chapter 11

§

MEDICAL SCIENCE FINDS
THE GOD IN YOU

*"Let me look on the world I see as the
representation of my own state of mind. I know
that my state of mind can change. And so I also
know that world I see can change as well."*

GOD-THROUGH-HELEN, (ACIM, W-P1.-54.2.:4-6)

As divine and glorious spiritual beings who are temporarily living in the physical realm, we require a physical body to move around in, interact with, and experience the physical environment. What is now becoming more apparent and validated through science is that our thoughts and beliefs play an equally large role in how we interact and experience this physical realm. The beliefs we hold about our own abilities, limitations, and fears can work to our advantage or disadvantage. Our thoughts and beliefs affect every aspect of our lives from achieving our dreams to improving our health. This is why it is critically important that we cast aside any belief that we are little and powerless in this world. Discoveries in medical science bring to light the extraordinary power and potential of the human mind, confirming once again the God residing in you.

THE MIND BODY CONNECTION

Spirituality has always said that we are three-part beings consisting of mind, body and spirit. Today, medical doctors acknowledge this natural connection. Recently, a close friend of mine had a visit to his doctor because he was suffering from a number of health related issues - high blood pressure, fatigue, loss of appetite, and a few other conditions. If his appointment had taken place six decades ago, the doctor may have started with a thorough examination, a battery of tests, followed by a diagnosis and most likely a prescription for some medication. I say this because six decades ago Western medicine didn't recognize the relationship between the mind and the body. At that time, the mind and the body were treated as completely separate parts. On my friend's recent visit to the doctor, his doctor listened intently as he explained the litany of ailments affecting him, and then the doctor asked him calmly: "What's going on in your life?" As it turns out, my friend was going through a very rough patch in his life, not only in his marriage, but also with his then teenage son who was battling a drug addiction and having run-ins with the law. Right away, the doctor recognized that his health aliments were related to the excessive stress in his life caused by his close relationships. We know now that unwanted stress lowers the immune response. I'm very happy to say that my friend's life has since turned around and although he's not in perfect health, he's now very happy and is looking like the person I remember him to be. The key here is that medical science now acknowledges this strong connection between the mind and body.

Hindsight is always twenty-twenty, but one wonders how and why medical science could have overlooked the mind-body connection when it's right there in front of us every day. Imagine for a moment that you're walking down a quiet, dimly lit street alone, late at night. The collar on your jacket is turned up because there's a chilly October cross wind blowing and the temperature is dropping steadily. You're not walking through a bad area of the city as such, but you know that crimes are committed every day in the city and you continue your walk through the night with a heightened vigilance, alert to anything out of the ordinary. Suddenly, looking ahead, you notice what appears to be a sinister figure peeking out at you from behind the lamp post - only ten meters in front of you! You stop abruptly, convinced that there is an attacker laying in wait behind the lamp post - you're sure that you've just seen him peek out! You're almost ready to turn and run the other way when you notice that it's not an attacker at all. It's just a plastic grocery bag that has become stuck to the lamp post and is flapping aimlessly in the wind. At times, it appears to be someone peeking out from behind the lamp post. You breathe an inner sigh of relief and continue on your way. We know that during this scenario, the thought of an attacker laying in wait initiated several physical responses in your body. As described in the last chapter, the "fight or flight" response is a naturally occurring reaction when we find ourselves faced with the apparent threat of danger. What does this tell us about the mind? It shows us that the mind can change the physiology of the body in a moment. In the scenario just described, there was never ever any sinister figure waiting for you behind the lamp post. There was only the thought of an attacker waiting for you behind the lamp post, and our thoughts are based solely in our minds. If someone should ask you to quickly change your physiology by dilating your pupils, altering your brain waves, changing the rate of your heart beat, and releasing extra adrenaline into your body, we're inclined to think that we're unable to do that; it's not possible. But our everyday experience clearly shows that we have this power to change our own physiology in an instant.[126]

WHAT THE PLACEBO EFFECT TELLS US

Even though the previous example shows the obvious connection between the mind and the body, medical science didn't identify the mind-body connection through our everyday experience. Instead, they actually stumbled upon it. The mind-body connection came to light through medical research studies involving placebos. If you're not familiar with what a placebo is, it's essentially a "fictitious cure" – it has no effect on the body. To study the healing effectiveness of a new drug, doctors would gather a group of patients suffering from the same physical ailment. Unbeknown to the patient group, some of them would receive the new experimental drug, while others would only receive a placebo. To the shock and bewilderment of the doctors conducting the study, they found that patients who were given the placebos were actually getting better. In some cases, the patients given the placebos were even better off than patients that had been given the new healing drug. This outcome, referred to as the "placebo effect", has occurred again and again through countless medical research studies. The late great Michael Talbot in his master work *The Holographic Universe* highlights several examples showing the power of the mind over the body. In some cases, doctors have even used surgery as a placebo to see if it would be effective in healing certain medical conditions. One such medical condition was "angina pectoris", which causes pain in the chest and left arm caused by a decreased blood flow to the heart. Back in the 1950s this medical condition was treated with surgery. A surgeon would operate on you and tie-off the mammary artery. To study the placebo effect, surgeons would operate on the patient but only cut them open and then sew them back up again without touching any of the coronary arteries. These studies showed that the patients who had the placebo surgery were also healed from their medical condition. In addition to angina pectoris, other conditions which have responded to the placebo treatment include migraine headaches; allergies; fever; the common cold; acne; asthma; warts; various physical pains; nausea and seasickness; peptic ulcers; psychiatric syndromes such as depression and anxiety; rheumatoid and degenerative arthritis; diabetes; radiation sickness; Parkinsonism; multiple sclerosis; and cancer.[127]

Talbot also reminds us that we experience the placebo effect in our everyday lives. Almost everyone knows someone who is sensitive to caffeine - they claim that the caffeine keeps them up at night. Studies have shown that persons claiming to be caffeine-sensitive will sleep quite soundly if they're given an injection of caffeine and told that it is a sedative to help them sleep. If an antibiotic has ever helped you to get over a lingering cold or sore throat, then you've experienced the placebo effect. All colds are caused by viruses, as are most types of sore throats, but antibiotics only fight bacterial infections and not viral infections.[128]

One rare psychological disorder is referred to "Multiple Personality Disorder (MPD)" or "Dissociative Identity Disorder

(DID)". Individuals experiencing this mental challenge exhibit two or more distinct personalities with distinct memories and behavior patterns for each personality. It's as if there are multiple unique individuals inhabiting the same body, in fact doctors, working in this field, sometimes refer to these individuals as "multiples". It is typical in these cases for the each personality in the multiple to have a unique name, age, artistic talents, language fluency, handwriting and IQ. The study of MPD patients gives untold insights into the human psyche, but they also show us the incredible potential of the human mind. Psychologists are still struggling to understand the causes and cure of this rare condition, and so there is still controversy in this field. However, what they have noticed is that the different personalities of the patient have different physical conditions. For example, one personality may suffer from diabetes, while the other personality shows no sign of diabetes but has an addiction to cigarettes. One personality has arthritis and the other personality has no sign of any arthritis. Doctors conclude that the mind of the patient is switching these physical conditions on and off like a light switch, depending on which personality comes to the forefront.[129]

So what is the significance and impact of the placebo effect? It is a resounding statement that each of us possesses the power to heal, at least to some extent, virtually all of our medical ailments and sicknesses. Oftentimes we are resigned in our belief that our sickness or disease will remain permanent for life. If we have arthritis, we believe it will never go away. If we experience migraines, then we accept it as part of life. We don't see the possibility that the situation could change by altering our thoughts and our beliefs. The studies into the placebo effect show undeniably that the healing power of the mind is there, but, as Talbot states, it's almost like we have to be "fooled" into using it. We haven't yet learned how to consciously harness and control this incredible mind power.[130] When Anita Moorjani was wheeled into the hospital emergency room with cancerous end-stage lymphoma, there was literally no hope. Even her attending physicians did not expect her to live through the night. But Anita makes a full and miraculous recovery and subsequently credits her defeat of the cancer to the new awareness of her spiritual magnificence and grandeur.[131] The placebo effect demonstrates another crucial factor about the mind: it doesn't distinguish between what is real and what we imagine or believe. What is it that changes in us when we receive a placebo? It's our belief about it - that's it. Where we were sick and ailing before, the only thing that has changed after we receive the placebo is our belief that we can now get better. The doctors know that the placebo has no healing effectiveness, but the placebo serves to change our belief and provide new hope that we can now recover from whatever is ailing us. In further contemplations, Talbot reasons that we may all be dormant Shaman or wonder workers who must now learn how to use the incredible power of the mind.[132]

> "Everyone experiences fear. Yet it would take very little right thinking to realize why fear occurs. Few appreciate the real power of the mind, and no one remains fully aware of it all the time. However, if you hope to spare yourself from fear there are some things you must realize, and realize fully. The mind is very powerful, and never loses its creative force. It never sleeps."[133]

God-through-Helen (ACIM, T-2.VI.9:1-6)

Dr. Jeanne Achterberg, PhD (1942 - 2012) and trained psychologist is credited with pioneering an innovative path of scientific research showing how "positive intent" is not only a medically sound course of treatment but also a necessary part of every healing process. Today an abundance of medical doctors are publishing books that teach people how they can heal themselves using their mind. Anita Moojani has recently published her own book entitled "Deep Meditation for Healing". Achterberg was the first to develop techniques teaching patients how to use imagery or visualization to heal themselves. In *Imagery in Healing*, one of her many books, Achterberg explains techniques for how patients could go about using mental images in their mind's eye to fight their disease or illness. For example, if you had a tumor, Achterberg's technique would correctly train your mind's eye to visualize your immune system breaking down the tumor and flushing it out of your body. This visualization exercise would be done multiple times per day, for a prescribed time, as long as the exercise was effective. Healing visualizations are really healing meditations designed to focus one's attention, promote a positive attitude, and change one's beliefs, but the crux of visualization therapy is to use the power of the mind to heal the body.[134]

Dr. Candace Pert (1946-2013) was an internationally recognized pharmacologist who published over two hundred and fifty research articles and was a significant contributor to the emergence of Mind-Body Medicine as an area of legitimate scientific research in the 1980s. Dr. Pert spent the better part of her career researching the mind-body connection. Among her other great accomplishments, Pert is credited with discovering the role of "neuropeptides" in the body. Neuropeptides are protein-like molecules in the brain which the brain uses to communicate. You can think of them as messengers passing information between your brain and other parts of the body. These messengers affect a wide range of brain functions including reward, appetite, metabolism, reproduction, social behaviors, learning, and memory - namely your immune system. Previous to this discovery, it was thought that neuropeptides only existed in the brain, but Pert discovered that there are receptors or receivers in our immune system that act as intakes for these neuropeptide molecules. In other words, our brain and immune system are in constant communication. In the past three decades an overabundance of medical studies have confirmed this by showing clear relationships between thoughts and illness. We know that hostile and aggressive individuals are seven times more likely to die from heart problems than non-aggressive, calm individuals; people with cancer live longer if they have a fighting spirit; pessimists get more colds than optimists; and people who've lost their spouse have more frequent incidence of illness and disease. This is a significant finding because it confirms what we've suspected for centuries. Our state of mind, our innermost thoughts and feelings, ultimately affect our health and well-being.[135] These findings also emphasize the critical importance of that inner dialogue that we carry on with ourselves each and every day. It's healthier for us to have positive, life-affirming thoughts, rather than negative life-denying thoughts.

SCIENCE SEES THE AMAZING HUMAN AURA

The human aura has been identified as a subtle energy field that surrounds each and every human being. I can't say that I've ever seen an aura myself, but it has been depicted in spiritual artwork for thousands of years, appearing as a colourful halo around a spiritual figure such as a prophet or a saint. Some talented psychics are able to see and read an aura, thereby supplying valuable insights about a person's mental state, emotional state, health, and a host of other aspects based on the colour, intensity, and clarity of the person's aura. In the NDE of Dannion Brinkley, profiled in chapter 3, Dannion talks about leaving his body while he was being driven to the hospital in the ambulance. During that time, his spirit is hovering above his lifeless body as the paramedics work feverishly to revive him. In that moment, Dannion notices the auras of his wife, close friend, and the ambulance attendants. Dannion describes the auras that he saw: *"As I watched my wife and Tommy, as they gave me CPR, for instance, I could see that they had certain shades of colors that the ambulance attendants did not have. They were the same basic colors, they were just shaded differently for each person. When I had my life review, I could see my own colors when I looked at my hands. Once again, the basic colors were the same as those in other people, they were just shaded differently for each person."*[136]

Medical science has long since known that we are beings with an electrical charge. Doctors look at the electrical activity of the heart with an electrocardiogram (EKG), and they also look at the electrical brain activity using an electroencephalogram (EEG). To measure the electrical activity of the muscles, doctors use an electromyography (EMG). Dr. Valerie V. Hunt, Ed.D. (1916 - 2014) was a pioneer in the area of bioenergy research. Dr. Hunt was responsible for ground-breaking research that led to the scientific understanding of the relationship between energy field disturbances, disease, and emotional illness. Hunt made her initial discoveries when she modified the EMG machine to measure the energy field of the human aura. She noted that aura energy, which she called the "human energy field", was smaller and more subtle than the other recognized body energy fields and instead of emanating from the brain, heart, or muscles, the human energy field was prevalent in the area of the body related to the chakras. Now, here's where it gets interesting: the next step in Hunt's research was to compare the different bodily energies with the newfound human energy. To Hunt's amazement and excitement, she found that the human energy responds to stimuli even before the brain does. To test this Hunt took readings from the modified EMG and the EEG readings of the brain simultaneously and discovered that reaction times to loud sound and bright light appeared on her modified EMG before they appeared on the EEG. In other words, the human aura would react to stimuli even before the brain.[137] The model of contemporary science tells us that the brain is first and the mind comes second, but reliable testimony from the NDE demonstrates otherwise. Now science itself is supporting a different view. The physical brain is not the seat of human consciousness as previously thought; rather, it is transforming and interpreting a signal from a higher entity - the God in you.

"What you call the mind is really an energy. It is...thought. And thought is an energy, not an object. Your brain is an object. It is a physical, biochemical mechanism - the largest, most sophisticated, but not the only - mechanism in the human body, with which the body translates, or coverts, the energy which is your thought into physical impulses. Your brain is a transformer."[138]

God-Through-Neale

SCIENCE MEETS SPIRITUALITY

One of the first (if not the first) scientist to really bring together science and spirituality is Dr. Gary E. Schwartz, PhD, a professor of psychology, medicine, neurology, psychiatry, and surgery at the University of Arizona and the Director of its Laboratory for Advances in Consciousness and Health. Dr. Schwartz was the first to apply the stringent guidelines of scientific experimentation to the readings of gifted psychic mediums. He has shown tremendous initiative and courage in working with gifted mediums within a scientific context. Later, in chapter 13, we'll talk more about gifted psychics, but for these experiments the gifted psychics involved are mediums. Unlike other psychics, the mediums are able to open up a communication channel between the physical realm and the spiritual realm, thereby allowing us to communicate with those who are now in the spiritual realm. For the first step, Schwartz enlists some random subjects who are referred to as "sitters" and some gifted mediums including the likes of John Edwards - the gifted psychic medium from the television show *Crossing Over*. The mediums then do readings for the various sitters and the percentage of accuracy is measured based on a correct answer. This would be a double-blind experiment, so the medium would not know who the sitter was and the sitter would not know who the medium was. The medium would then channel the spirit on the other side, asking the sitter questions to confirm the identity of the spirit. The sitter would never answer the medium directly, but would only nod their head to indicate a "yes" or "no" answer to a third party. Once the sitter had indicated their answer, the third party would, in turn, indicate to the medium if their answer was correct or not. This is the method used to test the accuracy of the mediums. All of the sessions were videotaped and audio recorded to ensure that the medium and sitter were not communicating directly in any way. Throughout these experiments Schwartz and team went to extreme precautions to eliminate the opportunity for fraud, cold reading, or lucky guesses - even consulting with a professional magician to expose any possible flaws in the experiment protocol. The accuracy of the mediums exceeded expectations, showing a high level of accuracy and confirming, from a scientific perspective, that human consciousness survives death.[139] All details about the experimental protocol and final results are well documented in Schwartz's book entitled *The Afterlife Experiments: Breakthrough Scientific Evidence of Life After Death.*

There is no doubt that many in the scientific community will always remain skeptical regardless of the evidence, but it's a start; we're moving in the right direction. Scientists will cringe at the thought of working with psychics, but Schwartz envisions a time when science and spirituality can work together to resolve some of our most perplexing problems.[140] Given what we know today about psychic abilities, this is not such a farfetched idea. What if the answers are waiting for us and we only have to ask?

For thousands of years our spiritual masters and spiritual teachings have told us about our unlimited potential and inherent power, but few of us really believe it. Most of us believe that we are much less than powerful beings, lacking the ability to change our life and create our reality. These scientific studies in psi and the mind-body connection reveal that we have a far greater potential to create our own reality than we could ever imagine.

Chapter 12

SCIENCE FINDS GOD IN THE UNIVERSE

"It has been said that ignorance is bliss. The truth is, it is often easier to hold on to the past than to face the discoveries revealed through science".

GARY E. SCHWARTZ, PhD, *THE AFTERLIFE EXPERIMENTS*

WE ARE CREATING OUR REALITY

When scientists first began to contemplate the origins of our universe, there was the widely accepted view in the science community that the universe and all its inhabitants were the lucky products of pure chance. That is to say that you and I came into being and are having the experience of the here and now by an arbitrary accident. It was taught and still a belief today that that entire universe, just one day, popped into existence - right out of nowhere.[141] For centuries, there was never any acknowledgement from the science community of an organizing, intelligent force behind the creation of the universe. However, scientists and researchers, by their nature, are an inquisitive bunch and they can't help but poke and prod at a scientific theory - even when it seems unchallengeable and airtight. With any long held scientific theory, you can be assured that some scientist or researcher, somewhere, is "kicking the tires on it", to satisfy an innate curiosity. When our scientists continue to look out into the universe and pore over the volumes of data from their telescopes and advanced space probes, they are forever learning more about the origins and nature of our vast universe. An intensive review of the data has had a tremendous impact on science and has divided the scientific community into two distinct groups. One group, that is rapidly losing support, holds tight to the belief that the entire universe is a product of chance happenings. The second group, whose support is steadily increasing, insists that the current available data confirms an intelligent designer behind the creation of the universe. This second group is still somewhat reluctant to use the "G-word" (God), but as scientists and researchers, they can't ignore the overwhelming evidence which science has revealed.

Some years ago, I was watching a televised scientific conference and the speaker was a well-known American politician and former presidential candidate. He was speaking to some prominent scientists in the Washington area. I thought that he made a very honest and profound statement when he said to the audience, "We know now that science is not about fact, science is about learning - that's why we have to change the text books every ten years." He was absolutely right. The view of the physical, mechanistic, process-oriented world that you and I learned about in our high school science class is rapidly becoming obsolete. The scientific model supporting the notion of an external world out there, separate and distinct from you and me, is being quietly set aside. The enduring scientific view that empty space between objects is inert and lifeless is seriously flawed. Even the once sacred and persuasive teachings of Darwin's Theory of Evolution have melted away under the microscope of scientific scrutiny. Although the remnants of these long held scientific views still fill our text books and are still taught in our classrooms today, there is a growing consensus that the models themselves are nearing their end of life and their place has already been reserved among the other timeworn relics in the museum of science history.

The renowned author, lecturer, and investigative journalist Mr. Lee Strobel was once an admitted hard-headed atheist. After enduring his own life crisis, he sets out on a quest to determine if his atheism is justified or not. Strobel, who credits his own atheism to his early interest and academic study of science, decides to put the question of God to some of the leaders in the scientific community. Through a series of one-on-one interviews with scientists who are considered leaders in their field of academic study, Strobel gets educated in the reasons why more and more scientists today view our universe as a product of intelligent-design. Strobel documents his story and his findings in his wonderful book entitled *The Case for a Creator: A Journalist Investigates Scientific Evidence That Points Towards God*. In this exploration of intelligent design, we look at some of the excerpts from the interviews.

SCIENTIFIC DISSENT FROM DARWIN'S THEORY OF EVOLUTION

Darwin's theory of natural selection told us that we all descended from one common ancestor, meaning that we were distant cousins to the giraffe, as well as the birds and the fish. Then, over millions of years, there were various genetic mutations taking place with new generations of species emerging and the once single species began to branch off into slightly different and unique species. Not all species could survive - only the ones whose genetic mutation afforded them some survival advantage over other species. The strongest of the species enjoyed survival while the weaker of the species perished - a process that Darwin called "natural selection". Gradually, through the ongoing process of genetic mutation and natural selection, an abundance of new species came into existence until we had the wide variety of species that we see today. I still recall sitting in science class and marveling over the illustration of Darwin's Evolutionary tree, showing how all the various animals had emerged from a single ancestor. At the time, it all seemed well researched and indisputable, but the truth is that today Darwin's Theory of Evolution is quickly losing the support and influence of the science community because there are just so many missing pieces to the puzzle[142].

When Darwin had formulated his theory of evolution, he knew that scientists would validate his theory using the fossils that they found. After all, if species were undergoing gradual and continuous transition, scientist would be able to see this in the fossils that they unearthed, often referred to as the "fossil record". In all fairness to Darwin, there were not a lot of fossils unearthed by paleontologists at the time, but Darwin and his supporters hypothesized that eventually, once explorations had greatly expanded, the fossils would be found and the fossil record would vindicate Darwin's Theory once and for all. Herein lies the biggest problem for Darwin's Theory of Evolution: after thousands of worldwide digs and wide scale explorations by paleontologists, the fossil record does not support Darwin's Theory. Scientists need to see tangible evidence, and in researching Darwin's theory, that evidence has not been forthcoming. What the scientists have found in the fossil record is something that is completely unexpected. The fossil record shows them that about five hundred and forty million years ago there was suddenly a flash flood of new species, what some paleontologists call the "Biological Big Bang" - ancestors for all the major groups of animals that we see today and some that have since become extinct, suddenly appear in the fossil record. Prior to this time, the primary life forms were spineless sea creatures like algae, jellyfish, and worms, and then suddenly you have some twenty to thirty-five completely new animal bodies. Since scientists can see that these new species came into being during the Cambrian Period, they refer to this event as the "Cambrian Explosion" and paleontologists consider it the single most spectacular phenomenon in the fossil record. The Cambrian explosion invalidates Darwin's Theory because the new species of animals have no ancestors. Instead, they have all the needed parts and they are fully developed and ready to go. This opposes Darwin's Theory that maintains that there are no sudden leaps and new species only come into being through a gradual transition taking thousands or millions of years.[143]

When we look at many similarities between animals and species, Darwin's Theory seems to make sense, but remember - at one time it appeared that the earth was flat and that we were physically at the center of the universe. Currently there are over a thousand very good and very reputable professors, laboratory researchers, and scientists across all scientific disciplines who are standing up to voice their opinion and sign their name in support of an online document called "A Scientific Dissent from Darwinism" (http://

www.dissentfromdarwin.org/). This online document contains one headlining statement that reflects their rigorous scientific investigation into Darwin's Theory of Evolution. Their statement reads, "We are skeptical of claims for the ability of random mutations and natural selection to account for the complexity of life. Careful examination of the evidence for Darwinian theory should be encouraged."[144] Although interesting, Darwin's Theory is considered by many scientist to be a fiction at best and does not explain the true origins of life on our planet. This is causing scientists to rethink and revise what they thought they knew and consider the possibility of intelligent design.

SOME REASONS BEHIND THE BELIEF IN INTELLIGENT DESIGN

In Strobel's investigation into Intelligent Design, the scientists present several examples of scientific evidence that point to an intelligent designer. In their explanations for intelligent design, one thing becomes crystal clear: these scientists have not been swayed by religious rhetoric, philosophical contemplations, or simply had a change of heart. Instead, these scientists, many of whom were previously atheist, have come to the rational conclusion of an intelligent designer through the scientific evidence produced in their work. The most significant scientific findings over the past six decades point toward a God - not away from God. Strobel's investigation focuses on six different fields of science namely; cosmology, astronomy, physics, biochemistry, biological information and human consciousness. This discussion would be far too lengthy if we were to look at each and every reason behind the position of these scientists, but here is the short answer. As our scientists look at the physical aspects of our universe and the complexity of life itself, they've learned there are an innumerable amount of physical conditions or parameters that must be in place to create and sustain a universe. In addition, there are even more conditions necessary to create and sustain life as we know it. Our scientists are not only astonished by the sheer volume of these necessary physical conditions, but they stand in absolute awe and amazement at the unimaginable precision and integration of all these very essential conditions.[145]

Dr. Patrick Glynn, PhD and author of *God: The Evidence*, was once a staunch atheist, but in studying the scientific evidence, he came across the "Anthropic Principle in Cosmology". This principle, in general, states the following: "All the seemingly arbitrary and unrelated constants in physics have one strange thing in common - these are precisely the values you need if you want to have a universe capable of producing life." For example, the Hubble telescope showed scientists that our universe was expanding - slowly moving outward. Scientists have also confirmed that the rate of that expansion is one part in a trillion, trillion, trillion, trillion, trillion. If that constant is changed by moving one part in either direction - a little faster or a little slower - we would not have a universe capable of supporting life. Another example is the range of forces that can be found in nature. The very weakest of the natural forces would be plain everyday gravity which you and I can experience on a daily basis. The strongest of the natural forces, a staggering ten thousand billion, billion, billion, billion times stronger than gravity, are the nuclear forces that bind together atoms and subatomic particles. Now, imagine these two extremes on a sliding scale - the weak force of gravity at one end and the incredible strength of nuclear force at the other end. This sliding scale is divided into inches and stretches across the universe, so that there are billions upon billions upon billions of inches on this scale. Scientists can see that the value for gravity occupies an extremely tiny range on this scale to facilitate life. If this gravitational constant is changed ever so slightly, by one inch, the impact for life in the universe would be catastrophic! That slight adjustment to the force of gravity would increase gravity a billion-fold, resulting in a universe that would not support life as we know it. I've very briefly described two of these physical constants found in our solar system and the universe, but there are over two hundred of these constants that we now know of. Recall that we are not even talking about all of the biological conditions required to support life; we're only talking about a universe that's able to support life. Not only are there over two hundred of these physical constants, but they all line up together. As our scientists discover the physics behind these constants including the incredible precision, the fine balancing, and the perfect alignment, it strains their imagination to presume that the universe is just a result of chance. On the contrary, a great many of our scientists and researchers have come to the rational conclusion that the constants have been carefully chosen and the universe has been fine-tuned by God to support life.[146]

One of the scientists interviewed by Strobel is Dr. Robin Collins, PhD, a leader in the field of physics and well-known author. Collins, once an atheist himself, has written several books in support of "intelligent design" such as *God and Design: The Teleological Argument and Modern Science; The Rationality of Theism;* and *God Matters: Reading in the Philosophy of Religion,* just to name a few. Collins explains the rationale this way:

"If I bet you a thousand dollars that I could flip a coin and get heads fifty times in a row, and then I proceeded to do it,

you wouldn't accept that. You'd know that the odds against that are so improbable - about one chance in a million billion - that it's extraordinarily unlikely to happen. The fact that I was able to do it against such monumental odds would be strong evidence to you that the game had been rigged. And the same is true for the fine-tuning of the universe - before you'd conclude that random chance was responsible, you'd conclude that there is strong evidence that the universe was rigged. That is designed."[147]

Similarly, when Neale questions God on the origins of our planet and the universe, God only confirms what our scientists are now concluding:

"The 'genetic stuff' of which you are made was placed on your planet, deliberately. It didn't just 'show up' there by accident. The elements that have formed your life didn't combine themselves through some process of biological serendipity. There was a plan involved. There is something much larger going on here. Do you imagine that the billion and one biochemical reactions it has taken to cause life as you know it to appear on your planet all occurred haphazardly? Do you see this outcome as simply a fortuitous chain of random events, producing a happy result by chance?"[148]

God-Through-Neale

Keep in mind that as a species we're still evolving in our awareness. Not only are we gaining an increasing awareness about ourselves, but we are also gaining awareness about our environment.

The new information and understanding of the universe is raising our consciousness about who we really are.

CONSCIOUSNESS IS EVERYWHERE

Since the days of the late great physicist Albert Einstein (1879 - 1955), scientists have discovered the very peculiar nature of solid objects. If you take an apparently solid object and continue to break it down into very tiny, microscopic pieces, you eventually come up with miniscule particles such as electrons, protons, and some other subatomic particles. Scientists refer to these tiny particles as "quantum particles" or simply "quanta". What's so startling to scientists is that these tiny particles do not possess the traits of normal objects that you and I know. With normal objects, scientists are able to measure their dimensions, predict their movements based on detailed calculations involving the object's present speed, weight, direction, and so on, but with quantum particles, these calculations and properties no longer apply. Another peculiarity about quantum particles is their dimensions. Typically, we're used to seeing an object with three dimensions, but again, this does not apply to quantum particles. For example, an electron has no width; scientists find it impossible to measure the width of an electron. The uniqueness of quantum particles does not end there. Another perplexing attribute that bewilders scientists is these quantum particles have a dual nature - sometimes they can appear as a particle and other times they appear spread out as a wave and can be in more than one place at a time.[149] If that wasn't enough, then the other extraordinary property of quanta is known as "entanglement". What scientists have discovered is that a pair of quantum particles (say two photons) that are created together continue to behave like they are not separated at all. Scientists will tell you that the two photons continue to share a wave function, so if one electron collapses into a wave, then the other electron will also collapse into a wave and if one electron changes its state to a particle, then the other electron also becomes a particle. The pair of electrons are forever in sync, as if they're in contact with one another and scientists have observed that this synchronization between pairs of quantum particles occurs instantaneously, even if the quanta are separated by a city block or across a universe. The synchronization of the quanta is not affected by time or space; in fact, the property of entanglement acts like there is no time or space and this is what so confounds our scientists and researchers who are studying quantum entanglement. If you think that this is some weird, very bizarre behavior for tiny particles, then you've got it; you're right on track - welcome to the world of quantum physics! The properties of quantum particles have perplexed scientists for decades. This information was staring back at our scientists when the great Albert Einstein was alive. Since that time, scientists have devised a number of ingenious experiments to test and confirm the properties of quantum particles and the experiments have been replicated successfully thousands of times in different laboratories. So what's the significance of quantum particles and their strange properties? Everything in the universe is made up of this stuff; everything has a particle nature and a wave nature - rocks, plants, stars, cell phones, you, and me. Anything that you can hold in your hand, no matter how dense, how heavy, how large, on its most fundamental level boils down to a collection of electric charges. Any and every object exhibits internal movement - everything.[150]

In laboratory experiments with quanta, scientists have discovered that the quanta react to the presence of consciousness. When

scientists or anyone for that matter observe the quanta in the laboratory, it causes it to change states, going from its wave form to its
particle form and remains in its particle form as long as consciousness is present. In the absence of consciousness the quanta returns
to its wave state. While in this wave state, one cannot tell when
and where the quanta will actually manifest as particle. Potentially
it could be any number of things, and for this reason, scientist
refer to the wave state as a "probability wave". When and where
the quanta manifest as a particle is completely dependent on when
the observer looks at it or when consciousness is present. The behavior and unique properties of these tiny particles is so odd to
scientists and researchers because it goes against all that they've
been taught about the behavior of solid objects in space and time.
How can a particle instantly form out of nothingness? How can
it be that nothing takes form until someone is looking at it? How
can a pair of electrons, separated by vast distances, stay in perfect
synchronization, acting like there is absolutely no space between
them at all? In the past scientists and researchers have avoided the
evidence for several decades, preferring to bite their tongue rather
than acknowledge that the universe has a consciousness. But all
that is changing.[151]

Today the literature is filling up with books based on new
scientific findings that point to the consciousness of the universe.
This quantum energy is in everything; it is even found in the
apparent empty space that surrounds us. The names vary. Some
call it "the field", others call it the divine matrix; and it's even
referred to by some as the "Holy Spirit", but they are all referring
to this universal consciousness found in quantum energy. Many
scientists believe this quantum energy is the medium that reacts
to our intentions, our beliefs, and our consciousness.[152] When

Anita had her near-death experience, one of her many insights that she gained was that the universe is infused with consciousness. Scientists studying this quantum energy believe that it acts as a medium allowing our inner thoughts to influence the physical world, as shown in the psi experiments, as well as transmit our thoughts, intentions, and feelings as demonstrated in the practice of prayer, remote viewing, and the REG machine experiments covered in chapter 10. We are totally immersed in this sea of quantum energy and it is the universal network responsible for the inter-connection between all things.

> "Everyone and everything on the planet - and in the universe - is emitting energy in every direction. This energy mixes with all other energies, criss-crossing in patterns of complexity beyond the ability of your most powerful computers to ana-lyze. The criss-crossing, intermingling, intertwining energies racing between everything that you can call physical is what holds physicality together. This is the Matrix, of which I have spoken. It is along this Matrix that you send signals to each other - messages, meanings, healings, and other physical ef-fects – created sometimes by individuals but mostly by mass consciousness."[153]

> God-Through-Neale

CONSCIOUSNESS IS EVEN FOUND IN WATER

Dr. Masaru Emoto has discovered that molecules of water are affected by our thoughts, words, and feelings. His findings are documented in his book entitled *The Hidden Messages in Water.*

Since humans and the earth are composed mostly of water, his message is one of personal health and global environmental renewal. As a child, Dr. Emoto had learned that no two snowflakes are the same. As Dr. Emoto pursued more serious studies, he discovered that no two crystals are the same either. In his subsequent laboratory work, Dr. Emoto decided to see if plain water was affected by music or human thought and if the effects could be seen in the crystals that the water formed. To conduct these experiments Emoto would expose the water to both positive and negative items, such as words, music, and even photographs for a set period of time. The exposed water was then frozen in petri dishes at -20°C (-4°F), for a period of three hours. As the ice began to melt, crystals emerged and could be photographed for only twenty or thirty seconds as the temperature rose. The results from these experiments were so astounding to Emoto and team that they could hardly believe what the crystals were showing them. Emoto believes that the information is so valuable and insightful that it's almost like a portal into another dimension. What Emoto found is that the water exposed to positive messages like "love" and "kindness" created beautiful, symmetrical, well-formed crystals. The water exposed to negative messages such as "fool" and "loser" created unattractive, malformed crystals. The most beautiful crystals came from water exposed to the positive words of "love" and "gratitude". The images of the crystals from Dr. Emoto's work can be found in his book or on the web if you google images of "Hidden Messages in Water". This is significant because both you and I are some 70% water, so we're much more affected by our environment and the people around us than we may be aware of.[154]

THE UNIVERSE IS INTERACTING WITH YOU

Earlier I mentioned that some scientists are now presenting new models of physical reality that include the element of human consciousness. One such scientist is Dr. Robert Lanza M.D., profiled earlier in chapter two. Lanza's radical new theory, called "Biocentrism", takes into account the inseparable relationship between human consciousness and quanta. The theory of Biocentrism, as Lanza explains in fine detail, shows that life creates the universe, not the other way around. Lanza is telling us that we are totally necessary in order to render a universe. If there were no consciousness, then there would be no world as we know it. We are creating the reality that we see and this is exactly what spirituality is telling us.[155]

> "Consciousness - a state of Being in which you grow until you reach full awareness, then becoming a True and Living God, creating and experiencing your own reality, expanding and exploring that reality, changing and re-creating that reality as you stretch your consciousness to new limits - or shall we say, to no limit. In this paradigm, Consciousness is everything. Consciousness - that of which you are truly aware - is the basis of all truth and thus of all true spirituality."[156]

> God-Through-Neale

The work of many dedicated scientists and researchers demonstrates our uniqueness in the universe, not as little inconsequential parts, but as very powerful spiritual beings who play an interactive role in creating our own realities. We are, in fact, affecting our environment more than we realize. All the science is not lessening us in any way; it's only reminding us of our true spiritual nature and grandeur. When our scientists look through their microscopes and telescopes, they're actually reading the clear messages quietly delivered by a loving and glorious God.

At this point you might be thinking to yourself, "Well, all the science may be interesting, but it still doesn't explain what life is for or why any of us are here at all." I hope you'll stay with me on this journey a while longer, as we look at some of the deeper questions about God and life in the final two chapters.

Chapter 13

YOU CAN'T STUB YOUR TOE IN HEAVEN

*"Well some say life will beat you down. Break
your heart, steal your crown. So I've started
out for God knows where. I guess I'll know
when I get there. I'm learning to fly."*

- Tom Petty and Jeff Lynn, *"Learning to Fly"*

THERE'S A SMALL PROBLEM WITH HEAVEN

The eye witness accounts from our NDErs, our contemporary messengers of God, and even our religions tell us that Heaven or the spiritual realm is beyond the description of any words. This is our natural home, filled with unspeakable beauty, amazing light, peace, tranquility, joy and overflowing with the exquisite, unconditional love of God. Everyone there is open, honest, respectful, kind, and loving.[157]

"Heaven is perfectly unambiguous. Everything is clear and bright, and calls forth one response. There is no darkness and there is no contrast. There is no variation. There is no interruption. There is a sense of peace so deep that no dream in this world has ever brought even a dim imagining of what it is."[158]

God-through-Helen (ACIM, T-13.XI.3:8-13)

If Heaven is so awesome and spectacular and I'm a glorious, godlike being of free will, then it begs the question: Why in the world would I ever leave Heaven and choose the earthly life I'm living now? Well, as wondrous as Heaven is, there are some things that we cannot experience there. For example, as a great spiritual being in Heaven, you can't have the experience of stubbing your toe. Heaven is pain-free, so you can't experience pain or any other kind of physical, mental, or emotional discomfort there - no one is suffering in Heaven. As spiritual beings, we can know about such things and fully understand them, but we can't actually have the experience of stubbing our toe. Only when you have a physical body in the physical realm and you unknowingly jam your bare toe into a rock or some other hard object protruding from the ground can you have the experience. You can't experience that unexpected, first numbing blow and the slow steady pain engulfing your toes and lower leg - you just can't have that experience in Heaven. Likewise, you can't experience loss and grief in Heaven because you always know exactly where everyone is and you can see them and be with them anytime. You can't experience fear in heaven either, because you're fully aware of your oneness with God and your immortal nature - you possess a profound understanding that you cannot be hurt, offended, or damaged in any way. Also, you can't experience feelings of littleness and separation from God in Heaven because you're completely aware of your spiritual magnificence and your inherent unity and close interconnection with all spirits. Neither can you have the experience of forgiving another person in Heaven, because there's no one in Heaven who would or could do something to hurt you. The negative emotions like hate and anger do not exist there. There are a multitude of experiences like these that can only be realized when we have a physical body in the physical realm with the forgetfulness of who we really are.

"At the outset, the idea was for you wonderful souls to have a chance to know your Selves as Who You Really Are through experiences gained in the physical body, in the relative world - as I have explained repeatedly here."[159]

God-through-Neale

WHY ARE WE HERE?

In my own humble opinion, the question, "Why am I here?" is being answered, not only by our contemporary messengers of God, but also by our gifted psychic mediums and by a lesser known spiritual researcher by the name of Mr. Robert Schwartz. While enduring his own life trials and struggles, Robert pursues his personal investigation into the meaning of life. Working with a team of four gifted psychic mediums (Ms. Deb Debari, Ms. Glenna Dietrich, Ms. Corbie Mitleid and Ms. Staci Wells), Mr. Schwartz seeks the answers to the questions that have eluded humanity since the beginning of time: Why does life have to be such a struggle at times? Why must I face deep personal disappointment? Included in Schwartz's investigation are ten individuals who have faced some major life traumas or setbacks such as drug addiction, alcoholism, loss of spouse, and critical illness. What does Schwartz uncover from this investigation? He discovers that our lives are not just random, pointless events in time, but they have purpose, structure, and meaning. As our NDErs also confirmed, there are no wasted lives, but each life brings us a step closer to spiritual mastery. In his fascinating and insightful book entitled *Your Soul's Plan: Discovering the Real Meaning of the Life You Planned Before You Were Born*, Schwartz and his team of gifted psychic mediums open a communication channel to the other side to converse with the spiritual guides who are overseeing the lives of individuals on earth. These spiritual guides confirm that our lifetimes are designed to give us spiritual growth and they involve a plan between us and other loved ones who voluntarily play a role in our current life.

WHAT IS A LIFE PLAN?

A life plan is essentially a blueprint for how we will "create" a life and obtain the spiritual growth and wisdom for ourselves as well as providing growth for others. We are all teachers and we are all students. The primary agenda of any life is to help ourselves through spiritual growth and be of service to others. Despite what you may be witnessing in your own life, Schwartz's investigation tells us that our life plans are carefully constructed. In these life planning sessions, we all have wise and loving spiritual guides who have been tasked with overseeing our spiritual growth and development by assisting us and guiding us in choosing the right life plan to obtain just the right spiritual growth that we will need at this particular time in our spiritual development. In addition to the input from our spiritual guides, we also collaborate with other souls who will join us in life and play a part in our growth. These other souls come into our life as our parents, our children, our siblings, our spouses, extended family members, friends, co-workers and even casual acquaintances.[160]

> "Other Players in the Universal Game join you from time to time – either as Brief Encounters, Peripheral Participants, Temporary Teammates, Long-Term Interactors, Relatives and Family, Dearly Loved Ones, or Life Path Partners. These souls are drawn to you by you. You are drawn to them by them. It is a mutually creative experience, expressing the choices and desires of both. No one comes to you by accident. There is no such thing as coincidence. Nothing occurs at random. Life is not a product of chance."[161]

God-through-Neale

Together we plan the events, circumstances and opportunities that are necessary to achieve the spiritual growth that we are seeking. Now, before you convince yourself that your life plan is not working, Schwartz reminds us that this plan is not like an earthly plan that we would create to build something or a project plan that you would come across in business and industry. Life plans are much more sophisticated than that; they are more like road maps. There are main highways, back roads, detours, short-cuts, meandering scenic routes, round-a-bouts, side streets, and exit points. There's no right or wrong route along this road; they're all a part of the same road. Nothing in this journey is scripted or set in stone, opportunities are created. The route we take and the time involved are entirely up to us based on the choices and decisions that we make along our life journey. In the planning stage we're able to look at the life plan and see how certain decisions and choices will result in certain consequences. The life plan is designed to take us to just the right events, circumstances and opportunities that will give us just the right experience that in turn leads to our spiritual growth and wisdom.[162]

> "The purpose is to create your experience - and thus, create your Self - in the glorious moment of Now. You do not therefore, choose the life you will experience ahead of time. You may, however, select the persons, places, and events - the conditions and circumstances, the challenges and obstacles, the opportunities and options - with which to create your experience. You may select the colours for your palette, the tools for your chest, the machinery for your shop. What you create with these is your business. That is the business of life."[163]

> God-through-Neale

Schwartz and team acknowledge that life plans are not a guarantee. Even the best laid plans can go off the rails. NDErs consistently return from the experience saying that it was not yet their time to die. Our lives are so vitally important that even if your physical body should die before your work is complete, there is no hesitation to send you back to your body. Most if not all the NDErs were told in one way or another: "Your work is not yet finished; you must return" or simply "Go back."

THE VITAL ROLE OF EARTHLY EXPERIENCE AND EMOTIONS

Our earthly experiences provide a mirror where we can know ourselves as who we really are. The experiences evoke feelings and emotions - feelings and emotions that we cannot experience in the spiritual realm. This is one of the main points that Schwartz and his team of gifted psychic mediums bring to light: we are obtaining spiritual growth and wisdom for ourselves, as well as others, through the feelings and emotions that we experience in life. We don't have to take Robert's word for it; just take a moment to reflect on your own life. Look at the defining moments that have shaped you and molded you into the person that you are today. Just look at your greatest personal struggles and problems to see how they have contributed to a wiser, enhanced You. You'll see that it was the emotionally-charged moments that have made you who you are now. If you're wondering what exactly spiritual growth is in this context, it is the increased capacity of your soul to possess the divine, virtuous traits of unconditional love, compassion, empathy, self-love, kindness, wisdom, power, dignity, humility, and many, many others. All of these are godly, magnificent traits that take us from being simply good Gods to spiritual masters. Therefore, the very fact that we chose to live a life is a declaration of our striving for spiritual mastery. In communication with the spiritual guides, Schwartz discovers that of all the divine spiritual traits, the ones that are most sought after through earthly experience are unconditional love, compassion, and empathy. We may not see or feel our life plan at a conscious level, but it stays with us at a subconscious level and occasionally spills over into our awareness in what we call déjà vu.[164]

The notion of a "life plan" can be very confusing, even inconceivable. We believe that given the opportunity to plan a life, surely we'd choose a life of ease, comfort, and luxury. This is the source of the confusion and it shows that we are still thinking in earthly terms or what Schwartz refers to as a "personality consciousness" as opposed to a "spiritual consciousness". Our spirit is already well aware of its immortal nature and the peace, beauty, and comfort of Heaven. Our spirit is seeking growth from earthly experience; this is why we chose to live a life in the first place. Let's look at a few examples of how life experiences lead to spiritual growth. Take something like critical illness: from an earthly perspective, you and I would never agree to take on a critical illness - who would want that? However, from a spiritual perspective there is opportunity for growth from critical illness. When you're critically ill, it brings spiritual traits to the forefront such as courage, faith, creativity, acceptance of opportunity, and compassion, just to name a few. It also brings new people into our lives who we would otherwise never get to know. These are traits that would lay dormant if we were otherwise perfectly healthy. We are all different and unique individuals, and we don't all learn or remember who we are under the same circumstances. Take a look at alcohol or drug addiction: from a personality perspective you'd never want that, but from a spiritual perspective, it's completely different. The alcoholic or drug addict is looked down upon by society and is often treated with little or no compassion. From the spiritual perspective the addiction creates an opportunity for that personality to expand their inner strength, overcome their addiction and learn to love themselves, improve their self-esteem, regain confidence, and eventually remember who they really are. Also, the addict becomes more sensitive to others who suffer from addiction and gains the compassion and empathy to help others who are suffering from an addiction. It also gives the people who are close to the addict a chance to move beyond judgment and gain tolerance and compassion. In this way the addict gives themselves and others an opportunity for spiritual growth. Many souls choose addiction for spiritual growth. At the very least, the addict creates the opportunity for others to grow through compassion, kindness, and unconditional love. As another example we could look at accidents and tragedy. From our earthly perspective, you'd never want any tragedy to befall you, your family, or your friends, but from a spiritual perspective the tragedy creates opportunities for spiritual growth through forgiveness, it also leads to changes that benefit all. The spiritual guides, communicating with us through gifted psychic mediums, tell us that many souls choose spiritual growth through accidents and tragedy.[165]

One of my favorite speakers was the late John Bradshaw (1933-2016). As an extraordinary speaker he really connected with his audience. In addition to speaking John Bradshaw had written several best-selling books with a focus on drug and alcohol addictions, recovery, codependency, and spirituality. His message has helped millions of people to become self-empowered and take control of their lives. If you ever got a chance to listen to John Bradshaw speak, he'd always talk about his dark past, growing up with an alcoholic father who abandoned the family when John was quite young. Despite the setback, he forged ahead and went on to become a very well-educated adult. Initially John had hoped to become a priest in the Catholic Church, but his plans to become a priest were hopelessly dashed when John himself became a chronic alcoholic. He will tell you that his life hit rock bottom the day he was wheeled into the emergency ward of the local hospital as a down and out alcoholic. This was a defining moment in John's life - a turning point when he made the decision to change his life. Who would have thought at the time that

John would use his battles with alcohol addiction to take his life to greatness? The alcoholism prepared him and gave him the expertise, inner strength, empathy, and compassion to counsel others who are struggling with addictions - the rest is history. John would not be the person he was without the alcohol addiction[166]. In this way, the alcohol addiction provided spiritual growth for John as well as the millions of people who have been uplifted and inspired by his message. This true life story also demonstrates how events and circumstances in our lives can be good and bad, right and wrong, a blessing and a curse, all at the same time.

> *"All events, all experiences have as their purpose the creating of opportunity. Events and experiences are opportunities. Nothing more, nothing less. It would be a mistake to judge them as "works of the devil," "punishments from God," "rewards from Heaven," or anything in between. They are simply Events and Experiences - things that happen. It is what you think of them, do about them, be in response to them, that gives them meaning."[167]*

> *God-through-Neale*

SPIRITUAL GROWTH THROUGH LOSS

The one experience that we will all have in this life is the experience of loss. During this short lifetime it is inevitable that someone close to us will pass away and move on. We're powerless to change the loss, but even in the tragedy of loss we can make the decision on how it will affect us. Jerry Sittser is professor of religion, holds a master of divinity degree from Fuller Theological

Seminary and a doctorate in history.[168] What you may not know about Jerry is that in this lifetime he's endured what can only be described as "catastrophic loss" when he lost three family members in a horrific automobile accident. Out of this tragic life event and circumstance, Jerry gives us a look inside at his inner turmoil, gradual transformation, wisdom, and realized spiritual growth in his very enlightening and deeply touching book entitled *A Grace Disguised: How the Soul Grows Through Loss*. The journey of Jerry's spiritual transformation begins on the day of the accident when he's returning home with his family and mother from a family day trip. To gain a real appreciation of what Jerry experiences and the shocking impact to his spirit, we need to hear his eyewitness account of the accident:

"By 8:15 p.m., however, the children had had enough. So we returned to our van, loaded and buckled up, and left for home. By then it was dark. Ten minutes into our trip home I noticed an oncoming car on a lonely stretch of highway driving extremely fast. I slowed down at a curve, but the other car did not. It jumped its lane and smashed head-on into our minivan. I remember those first moments after the accident as if everything was happening in in slow motion. They are frozen into my memory with a terrible vividness. After recovering my breath, I turned around to survey the damage. The scene was chaotic. I remember the look of terror on the faces of my children and the feeling of horror that swept over me when I saw the unconscious and broken bodies of Lynda, my four-year-old daughter Diana Jane, and my mother. I remember getting Catherine (then eight), David (seven), and John (two) out of the van through my door, the only one that would open. I remember taking pulses doing mouth-to-mouth resuscitation, trying to save the dying and calm the living. I remember the feeling of panic that struck my soul as I watched Lynda, my mother, and Diana Jane all die before my eyes. I remember the pandemonium that followed – people gawking, lights flashing from emergency vehicles, a helicopter whirring overhead, cars lining up, medical experts doing what they could to help. And I remember the realization sweeping over me that I would soon plunge into a darkness from which I might never again emerge as a sane, normal, believing man."[169]

As if the devastating loss was not enough, Jerry learns that this completely random accident was caused by a drunken driver. With the subsequent trial that followed, Jerry was looking forward to his day in court when he would gain an iota of satisfaction, justice, and revenge for the heinous crime that had been committed against him and his family, but this was not to be the case. In a shocking turn of events, Jerry's attorneys had become too complacent, thinking that this was a simple open-and-shut case. They hadn't prepared properly in building a solid case against the driver. The skillful legal moves of a well-prepared defence attorney got all the charges dropped and the drunk driver was allowed to walk out of the courtroom a free man.[170] It's very difficult to imagine the immeasurable pain and suffering brought on by this catastrophic life event, but Jerry's is not a story of healing or a story of how his life would return to some form of normalcy. Instead, it is the story of how he learned to cope with this life tragedy after the accident and allowed it to transform and grow his spirit. He still remembers and wishes that the accident never happened. He still misses his mother, wife, and young daughter very, very much, but as strange as it sounds there is some good that comes out of this life experience for Jerry's spiritual growth. Even with this travesty of justice he finds the inner strength to forgive the driver of the accident:

"Unforgiveness uses victimization as an excuse. Unforgiving people become obsessed with the wrong done to them and are quick to say, "You don't know how unbearable my suffering has been! You don't know how much that person hurt me!" They are, of course, right. No one can know. But I wonder sometimes if being right is worth all that much. Is it worth the misery it causes? Is it worth living in the bondage to unforgiveness? Is it worth the cycle of destruction it perpetrates?"[171]

Through Helen God provides this perspective on forgiveness:

"Remember that in every attack you call upon your own weakness, while each time you forgive you call upon the strength of God in you."[172]

God-through-Helen (ACIM, W-P1.62.3:1)

In communication with spiritual guides, our gifted psychics frequently use the word "opportunity" to describe the purpose behind events, struggles, accidents, and circumstances in our lives. In this context, opportunity refers to the potential for new spiritual growth and wisdom. In Jerry's case, as with many tragic accidents, he's given the opportunity for forgiveness. He will be the first one to tell you that forgiveness does not always come easy, but is a slow, drawn out process that can take an entire lifetime. His pain is transformed into a new inner strength allowing him to cope with anything life can throw at him. His faith and relationship to God has been strengthened. Last but not least, Jerry gains a new level of compassion and empathy for others who experience loss in life. Three years after this tragedy, Jerry can feel the transformation of his spirit:

"Above all, I have become aware of the power of God's grace and my need for it. My soul has grown because it has been awakened to the goodness and love of God. God has been present in my life these past three years, even mysteriously in the accident. God will continue to be present to the end of my life and through all eternity. God is growing my soul, making it bigger, and filling it with himself. My life is being transformed. Though I have endured pain, I believe that the outcome is going to be wonderful."[173]

Chapter 14

LIVING THE LIFE OF YOUR CREATION

"For nothing happens by accident in God's world,
and there is no such thing as coincidence.
Nor is the world buffeted by random
choice, or something you call fate."

GOD-THROUGH-NEALE, *CONVERSATIONS WITH GOD: BOOK 1*

OUR LIFE CHALLENGES

As long as we continue to view life with an earthly perspective, events such as "tragic accidents" will never make any sense. The accident only appears that way from our earthly perspective, but there are no "accidents" in God's perspective. We are all very courageous beings, and although we may not recall giving our consent, we take up these life challenges to grow in spirit and to help others grow in spirit. Earlier, back in chapter 9, I mentioned Mr. Roy Mills, a man who is gifted with remembering his pre-birth life in Heaven. With his unique gift, Roy explains beautifully the role of our life challenges:

> *"In Heaven, everyone who chooses to be born on earth is thought of as a courageous spirit. It's not easy to leave the peace and love of Heaven for the hardships and strife of earth. During our time here, we all have something to overcome: a challenge we have chosen to help us grow. Worry, low self-esteem, relationship problems, pride, anger, selfishness, greed, addiction, fear, and negative thinking are only some of the personal problems that can control us and keep us from true happiness. I was told that many people live with their personal problems so long that they sometimes just accept them. They say to themselves "That's just part of who I am. I can't change it." But this is the result of earthbound thinking. While in Heaven, we didn't choose these problems because we wanted to live with them. We chose them because we wanted to grow by overcoming them. God doesn't want us to merely endure hardship; He wants us to learn from it and find happiness."*[174]

I know this will be very difficult for some of us to accept and I don't mean to be insensitive or disrespectful to Dr. Sittser or the Sittser family, but the existence of life plans would imply that Jerry's catastrophic accident was part of a plan. Knowing the deep love and wisdom of his spiritual guides, you can be assured that Jerry and the spirits of his immediate family were warned and well advised about taking on a life challenge with this degree of difficulty. Included in Jerry's life plan and taking an active role are the loving and courageous spirits of Jerry's wife, his mother, children, and others, including the driver of the other car. It is often the case that spirits collaborating on a life plan share an extremely strong bond of love and have worked together before in creating a life plan.[175] Schwartz offers these insights about earthly accidents:

> *"Sometimes, short lives are chosen when a soul wishes to accelerate its growth. We ask you to know that there are no simple answers. All lives are interconnected. This is a basic spiritual tenant. So, to ask did A happen simply because of B - no, it happened because of B, B prime, C and many other reasons. This is why planning is required before incarnation - to make sure that the life weavings benefit all for the lessons they wish to learn."[176]*

We choose just the right conditions and circumstances to insure we obtain the spiritual growth that we are seeking.

> *"You choose everything. Your parents. Your country of birth. All the circumstances surrounding your re-entry. Similarly, throughout the days and times of your life you continue to choose and to create people, events, and circumstances designed to bring you the exact, right, and perfect opportunities you now desire in order to know yourself as you truly are."[177]*

> *God-through-Neale*

Life challenges refer to the obstacles and circumstances that we must overcome in order to realize our spiritual growth. To gain a fuller understanding of life challenges, let's look at how some souls would plan a life and choose specific challenges to foster their own spiritual growth and help others to grow also. Spiritual growth through life challenges can take a number of different forms. For example, as a spiritual being you may choose a lifetime to develop your inner strength and faith. Again, we are all unique beings, so the challenges we select to obtain spiritual growth may be different from one spirit to the next. In this case, the spirit decides to accomplish inner strength through their relationship with their parents. In the developing of a life plan, the spirit engages another loving spirit to play the role of a judgmental and demeaning father. The spirit insists that the father figure shame him, beat him down and disrespect him, so that the opportunity is created for the spirit to gain inner strength through overcoming this challenge and expand their self-esteem and will. Once the spirit takes on the life and begins to live out their life plan, it is completely up to them. When confronted with the life choices and opportunities, the personality may choose to rise to the challenge and build their inner strength, or they may have another opportunity with a spouse, partner, co-worker to obtain the level of spiritual growth that they were seeking.[178] Schwartz also points out that even those who mistreat us are actually engaged in a form of service. Illness too offers opportunities for the ill person and the one caring for the ill person. Although it may seem burdensome to be the one who is ill or caring for the one who is ill, it is a stepping-stone to something else. It is a rung on the ladder of evolvement.

Roy Mill clearly remembers his own life planning session with his spiritual guides. The session begins with Roy's guides showing him a scroll that depicts various life challenges and the growth they will bring. Roy recalls the discussion with his guide:

"'We are going to help you choose your life experiences,' he told me. 'The things you choose here will come to pass after you are born. They will help you and others grow in spiritual knowledge

and wisdom.' The scrolls were filled with descriptions of all types of experiences, and the angels discussed each of the possible choices with me. They told me what each would involve and how it would help me grow or help others grow. They explained that the more difficult a challenge was, the more knowledge and wisdom and love it could bring. I knew that it would be pleasing to God if I dealt with many experiences in a positive way, so I began selecting all kinds of challenges. I suppose I was like a kid in a candy store, and the angels finally warned me that I was choosing too many challenges for one lifetime. They strongly advised me to shorten my list, and I reluctantly did."[179]

As I said before, we're all very courageous spirits to consent to the hardship of a physical life. Now, let's say that you're a very courageous and determined spirit who adamantly chooses spiritual growth through physical illness because it offers you just the right kind of spiritual growth that you're seeking at this time in your spiritual development. Your loving and compassionate spiritual guides who are overseeing your spiritual development implore you to take more time to consider this decision of taking on such an arduous life challenge, but still, you're adamant. Your guides then strongly advise you to take a waiting period to contemplate your commitment to this life challenge. You reluctantly take their advice and after the waiting period, you are steadfast in your determination to take on this life challenge and achieve the spiritual growth it offers. Sometime later, your guides take you aside and ask you to reconsider your options in light of the difficult demands of this life challenge, but still, you're insistent that you are prepared and want to take on this life challenge. Finally, you are permitted to live this life and your life plan is now settled. You take on a physical life and live your life just as you've planned. You take birth, grow up and then the day comes in your life when you're stricken with the physical illness and you are petrified. You do not remember that you are a God and that you are immortal, so both you and your family pray with all your heart to be healed of the illness. After completing all the perquisites, the waiting involved and the demonstrated commitment what are your guides supposed to do? If God and your spiritual guides should intervene and heal you of the illness, they would be essentially ruining the entire life that you had planned for yourself - what are they supposed to do?[180] The concept of life planning also tells us that physical and mental disabilities are not the result of "bad genes", inherited disorders, or "sins passed on from the parents". In each case the determined, magnificent spirit has simply chosen a different set of circumstances to live this particular life for their own spiritual growth and the spiritual growth of others. Again, Roy Mills provides further insights:

"Some spirits choose a life of extreme sacrifice of nearly unbearable suffering. The light of God shines brightly around these people, and in Heaven they are thought of as mighty spirits because they come to earth to suffer so that others can grow in understanding and love. Some mighty spirits choose to be born with severe disabilities such as blindness, deafness, mental illness, Down's Syndrome, and others. Some choose to be paralyzed or disfigured or disabled later in life by an accident. Others suffer a life-threatening illness such as cancer or Alzheimer's. And many brave spirits choose to be born into alcoholic or drug-addicted families, or into abusive homes where they suffer and sometimes even die from abuse. Many of these people who suffer from such challenges live their lives thinking they are inferior or unworthy of love because they look different or don't have the same abilities as most people, or

because they were the victims of abuse. But the truth is that they are mighty spirits who denied themselves and have come to earth to help others grow."[181]

It's incredible to acknowledge the life challenges that some of us willingly accept. It exemplifies the love that we have for each other.

"In other words, no one is "disadvantaged," given what the soul wishes to accomplish.

For example, the soul may wish to work with a handicapped body or in a repressive society or under enormous political or economic constraints, in order to produce the conditions needed to accomplish what it has set out to do. So we see that people do face "disadvantages" in the physical sense, but that these are actually the right and perfect conditions metaphysically."[182]

God-through-Neale

Some spirits possess such an abundance of love and compassion for others that they take on onerous life challenges of the highest degree. These spirits are easy to recognize because when you and I look upon them, we are immediately reminded of our many blessings and the trivial nature of our own so called "problems". They evoke sympathy and compassion from even the most hardhearted of us. Roy gives us a spiritual perspective on these individuals:

"When we see a child who is confined to a wheel chair because of a problem with his or her muscles or nerves or brain, we feel

compassion for the child. But the deeper truth is that this individual had compassion for us first, having chosen their condition to help us grow. When we think we are helping the disabled, we are really helping ourselves by learning selflessness, charity, and how to demonstrate our love."[183]

The spiritual perspective changes everything for me. My own dear sister, who I'll refer to as Mel, has struggled with mental health and drug addiction for most of her life. Growing up as a young woman Mel caused plenty of heartache to the family and I went through stages of distancing myself from her. My mother and I both prayed for Mel's healing, always hoping that, by some miracle, Mel would return to the person that we once knew. Yet now, growing older and wiser, I see Mel and her life quite differently. Knowing that there are no accidents in God's world and everything has a reason, I see Mel as a very loving spirit who agreed unselfishly to live her life in such a way so that I may have the opportunity to grow my spirit with compassion, mercy, unconditional love, tolerance, non-judgment, and forgiveness. It has also given me more compassion for others who suffer from mental health issues as well as their family members.

I look at Ms. Caitlyn Jenner, a very famous and popular person who changed their sexual identity in front of the entire world, and I see a gracious and compassionate spirit of tremendous inner strength and courage. The spirit of Caitlyn Jenner has taken on a monumental life challenge of giving all of us the opportunity to experience unconditional love, tolerance, mercy, non-judgment, and even forgiveness. It's natural to question this spiritual perspective and the notion of a life plan, but at some level, we already recognize this wisdom. We use old clichés like, "What doesn't kill you, just makes you stronger" or "Whatever happens, happens for the better" or "Everything happens for a reason" or another popular favorite: "No pain, no gain."

Back in late 2015 when Syrian refugees were very desperately fleeing their country to escape the horrifying war there, a little three-year-old boy fell from an overcrowded boat during a violent storm. Later, his small lifeless body was washed ashore on a beach in Turkey. The photographs of this tragedy went viral throughout the world on social media, newspapers, and television. Almost immediately, countries that had previously resisted accepting Syrian refugees opened their doors to welcome them in with arms wide open. The news and images showing the little boy lying on the beach invoked compassion in all of us. That little boy's death was not in vain. He gave us all the opportunity to experience compassion and mercy, and to take a more humane approach to assisting those that are in desperate need of our help. We should be grateful to that little boy for allowing us to grow our spirit through compassion. God shows us too, how one life can be used to change many lives. Schwartz tells us that in many ways, this lifetime is a journey that encourages us to think more with our hearts than with our heads.[184]

> "Your potential is unlimited in all that you've chosen to do. Do not assume that a soul which has incarnated in a body which you call limited has not reached its full potential, for you do not know what that soul was trying to do. You do not understand its agenda. You are unclear as to its intent. Therefore bless

every person and condition, and give thanks. Thus you affirm the perfection of God's creation and show your faith in it."[185]

God-through-Neale

Schwartz and his team remind us that the question is not, "Did I ask for this challenge in my life?" but rather, "Why do I have this challenge in my life?" At the spiritual level, there is no pass or fail in life or "badness" in the experience; there is only choosing your lesson.[186] Like in the case of the late John Bradshaw overcoming the life challenge results in our spiritual growth. This newfound spiritual growth gives us inspiration and motivation to effectively help others. Just look at the founders of the various self-help groups, that were inspired to help others as a result of their own life challenges; The founder of Alcoholics Anonymous (AA) was himself a chronic alcoholic. The founder of MADD (Mothers Against Drunk Drivers) lost a child in an accident caused by a drunken driver. The founder of Prison Fellowship, an organization that serves prison inmates and their families, spent time in prison. The founder of the Breast Cancer Research Foundation, was herself diagnosed with early stage breast cancer. [187] The tragedy, the accident, and the struggles are like rays of sun that shine in through the forest canopy and pour over the dormant plant on the forest floor, allowing it to grow and blossom fully into its true magnificence. Robert Schwartz sums up this new spiritual perspective of life:

"As we expand our self-concept from personality to soul, we grant ourselves a more accurate self-understanding. We also shift our focus from the pain caused by life challenges to the wisdom and

growth they offer. When we saw pointlessness, now we see purpose. When we saw a punishment, now we see a gift. When we saw burden, now we see opportunity. Never again the victims of life, we become the recipients of its many blessings."[188]

Watch your kids or nephews or nieces grow up, watch your parents pass away, and watch your favorite entertainers, actors, athletes, comedians and musicians pass on. This lifetime is short, and any pain or suffering we experience is really only very temporary. Realize that the spiritual growth we obtain lasts for eternity.

Summary

WALKING IN AWARENESS

*"Yet as you watch your own life roll out before you, do
not yourself become unraveled. Keep your Self together!
See the illusion! Enjoy it! But do not become it.
You are not the illusion, but the creator of it.
You are in this world, but not of it".*

GOD-THROUGH-NEALE, CONVERSATIONS WITH GOD: BOOK 3

Today our contemporary messengers of God, our gifted psychics, our near-death experiencers, and even our scientists are confirming that we are and always will be divine spiritual beings on a spiritual journey to mastery. Of our own free will, we are striving to grow and expand our magnificence through choosing an earthly life filled with deliberate challenges, opportunities and events that will ultimately lead to greater spiritual growth for us and for other spiritual beings who we meet along the way. As a part of this journey, you and I willingly submit to a temporary amnesia, a forgetfulness of who we really are and where it is that we come from. Once again, Schwartz and team reiterate that this forgetfulness and the illusion of separation from God is necessary in order to provide rich life lessons. Otherwise life would lack the potency to be our teacher and we wouldn't have the motivation to be life's students.[189] The message in Part One is to remind us of a God of unconditional love and the true nature of who we really are - magnificent spiritual beings created in the very likeness of God. Although we experience the feeling of being separate and apart from God, we know that we are never apart from God and God is never apart from us. If anyone should ever ask you about your family lineage or the origins of your family ancestry, let them know, honestly and openly, that you are a direct descendant of God. You are nothing less than that.

> "Let go all the trivial things that churn and bubble on the surface of your mind, and reach down and below them to the Kingdom of Heaven. There is a place in you where there is perfect peace. There is a place in you where nothing is impossible. There is a place in you where the strength of God abides."[190]

God-through-Helen (ACIM, W-P1.47.7:3-6)

Life events, opportunities, and circumstances exist to create opportunities for spiritual growth. We can only experience compassion if someone creates that opportunity for us. We can only experience selflessness when someone creates that opportunity. Life is not consisting of pointless suffering. Although the experiences can be painful, they are transforming us forever. In remembering who we are, we must remember who everyone else is too. Due to our unique nature, we don't always obtain spiritual growth in the same way. Some of us choose to obtain compassion by caring for others or helping others that are less fortunate. Some of us are willing to devote entire lifetimes to helping others in their spiritual growth. One could choose to increase their inner strength by overcoming life challenges in oppression, hard work, illness, physical or economic disadvantage. Even that person we imagine to be lowly and unworthy of our love and respect is a divine and magnificent spiritual being - just like you. This translates into giving respect for everyone and recognizing that they too are walking their own spiritual path to mastery.

> "But when you look upon a person as a physical entity, their power and glory are 'lost' to you and so are yours. You have attacked them, but you must have attacked yourself first."[191]

> God-through-Helen (ACIM, T-8.VII.5:3,4,)

Our lives are very important, so much so that we will have a full life review once we complete this lifetime and return to the spiritual realm. There are no "wasted" lives per se, but we understand now that there is missed opportunity to obtain spiritual growth. We know too that God is a God of unconditional love and forgiveness, a God who would never send us to eternal Hell and damnation, even if such a place existed and it does not. The ending of this life is not the end of us - we are immortal. As this life ends, so another begins and we continue on in a new life and a new adventure. Given what we know about God and life today, it becomes most obvious that this earthly life is more of an illusion than a reality. Many of our scientist and researchers are confirming this now.

"Even the illusion you can then enjoy. For you will know it is an illusion, and that is half the enjoyment! It is the fact that you think it is real that causes you all the pain. Nothing is painful which you understand is not real."[192]

God-through-Neale

Here is one common illusion that we are all subjected to and it all begins when we are new infants born into earthly life. It all starts when we are told, at a very early age, that we are small and little. As we grow up into adults, when there's something that we can't do, or something that we don't have, or something that we don't know, we tell ourselves that we are still small and little. We may even feel that we are inferior to others. On the other hand, because there is something that we can do, or something that we do have, or something that we do know, we tell ourselves that we are no longer small and little. On the contrary, now we are very, very big and we may begin to believe that we are superior to others. These are just illusions rooted in the belief that we were once small and little. Yet the truth is we've never been small and little; we've only ever been and continue to be magnificent, divine Gods on a spiritual journey of growth.[193] This lifetime is only a very short period, but the spiritual growth we obtain lasts for an eternity.

"To accept yourself as God created you cannot be arrogance, because it is the denial of arrogance. To accept your littleness is arrogant, because it means that you believe your evaluation of yourself is truer than God's."[194]

God-through-Helen (ACIM, T-9.VIII.10:8,9)

As we continue this journey of spiritual growth, we will someday reach a stage in our own spiritual development when we no longer have a need to live an earthly life in the physical realm with a physical body. There will soon be a time when you and I will work as wise, loving, and compassionate spirit guides to help others in their ongoing spiritual development. This is a continuous journey that unfolds in amazing ways which we can't even begin to imagine.

> "Even the rock will not be a rock forever, but only what 'seems like forever.' Before it was a rock, it was something else. It fossilized into that rock, through a process taking hundreds of thousands of years. It was once something else, and will be something else again. The same is true for you. You were not always the "you" that you are now. You were something else. And today, as you stand there in your utter magnificence, you truly are....'Something else again.'"[195]

> God-through-Neale

Thanks to our contemporary messengers of God; the near-death experiencers; the gifted psychics; our ancient spiritual teachers; and the contribution from our scientists, medical doctors, and researchers we have the more evidence about God and life today than ever before. This evidence was simply not available a fifty years ago. God does not "move in mysterious ways", but has a phenomenal plan in place for each and every one of us. God is using life to transform and forge us into masterful and amazing Gods. All of this to position us for the next phase of the unending journey of spiritual growth and fulfillment.

It's my hope that you will join me again for part two of "Relax… You're Not Going to Die", where we will continue the discussion of life plans and more insights from the other-side. We'll also look at ways to bring more spirituality into our lives and finally some spiritual advice to help us achieve our life dreams. Thank so much for reading this.

ABOUT THE AUTHOR

Darryl Philip, is an information technology professional, a self-taught and God inspired theologian researching spiritual truths and the purpose of life.

A seeker of purpose and life's rationale since his teen years, Philip's passion to find the answers about life led him to completely immerse himself in the study of spiritual enlightenment. He has devoted his career to finding simple answers to life's most complex questions, many of which have been thought unanswerable.

Through diligent investigation—attending religious seminars, reviewing contemporary sermons, researching near-death experiences, perusing developments in science and medicine, listening to the acclaimed psychics, and digging up the facts on ancient beliefs—he remains dedicated to the idea that uncovering God's incredible plan for us is an attainable goal.

ENDNOTES

1. Moody, Raymond A. Jr, *"Life After Life"*, New York, NY, Published by Bantam Books in arrangement with Mockingbird Books, 1975

2. Tutu, Desmond, *"Time Magazine Special: Discovering Heaven: How Our Ideas About The Afterlife Shape How We Live Today"*, New York, Ny, Published by Time Magazine, June 2014, pg 74.

3. Guggenheim, Bill and Guggenheim Judy,"Hello From Heaven!", New York, New York, Bantam Books. 1995, pg 19

4. Guggenheim, Bill and Guggenheim Judy,"Hello From Heaven!", New York, New York, Bantam Books. 1995, pg 13

5. Guggenheim, Bill and Guggenheim Judy,"Hello From Heaven!", New York, New York, Bantam Books. 1995, pg 21

6. Walsch, Neale Donald *"The New Revealations: A Conversation With God"*, New York, New York: Atria Books, 2002, pg 312

7. Walsch, Neale Donald *"The New Revealations: A Conversation With God"* New York, New York: Atria Books, 2002, pg 153

8. Walsch, Neale Donald, *"Conversations With God: An Uncommon Dialogue, Book 3"*, Charlottesville, Virginia: Hampton Road Publishing Company, 1998 pg 6

9. Walsch, Neale Donald, *"Conversations With God: An Uncommon Dialogue book 1 Hardcover"*, New York: G.P. Putman's Sons, 1996, pg 1

10. Schuman, Helen and Thetford, William "A Course In Miracles Third Edition" Mill Valley, California: Foundation For Inner Peace, 2007, pg Preface vii

11. Schuman, Helen and Thetford, William "A Course In Miracles Third Edition" Mill Valley, California: Foundation For Inner Peace, 2007, pg Preface viii

12. Parnia, Sam. *"What Happens When We Die"*. New York, New York: Hay House Inc., 2006, pg 9-10

13. Long, Jeffery, *"Evidence of the Afterlife: The Science of Near-Death Experiences"*, New York, New York, HarperCollins Publishers, 2011, pg 65-68

14. Long, Jeffery, *"Evidence of the Afterlife: The Science of Near-Death Experiences"*, New York, New York, HarperCollins Publishers, 2011, pg 53

15. Eadie, Betty J., *"Embraced By The Light"*, Placerville, California: Green Leaf Press, 1992, pg 1

16. Eadie, Betty J., *"Embraced By The Light"*, Placerville, California: Green Leaf Press, 1992, hardcover pg 28-29, 34

17. Ring, Kenneth and Cooper, Sharon, *"Mindsight: Near-Death and Out-of-Body Experiences in the Blind"*, Bloomington, Indiana, iUniverse Inc., 2008, pg 12

18. Lanza, Robert,"*Biocentrism: How Life and Consciousness are the Keys to Understanding the True Nature of the Universe*", Dallas, Texas, BenBella Books Inc., 2010, pg 21

19. Ring, Kenneth and Cooper, Sharon, *"Mindsight: Near-Death and Out-of-Body Experiences in the Blind"*, Bloomington, Indiana, iUniverse, pg 80.

20. Brinkley, Dannion, *"At Peace in the Light"*, New York, New York, HarperCollins Publishers, 1996, pg 37

21. Morse, Melvin L.,"*Closer To The Light: Learning From the Near-Death Experiences of Children*", New York, New York, Ivy Books, 1990, pg 190-191

22. Morse, Melvin L.,"*Closer To The Light: Learning From the Near-Death Experiences of Children*", New York, New York, Ivy Books, 1990, pg 204

23. Lanza, Robert, *"Biocentrism: How Life and Consciousness are the Keys to Understanding the True Nature of the Universe"*, Dallas, Texas, BenBella Books Inc., 2010, back of book

24. Lanza, Robert, *"Biocentrism: How Life and Consciousness are the Keys to Understanding the True Nature of the Universe"*, Dallas, Texas, BenBella Books Inc.,2010, pg 191

25. Moody, Raymond A. Jr, *"Life After Life"*, New York, NY, Published by Bantam Books in arrangement with Mockingbird Books, 1975, pg 183.

26. Neal, Mary C., "To Heaven and Back: A Doctor's Extraordinary Account of Her Death, Heaven, Angels, and Life Again", Colorado Springs, Colorado, WaterBrook Press, 2011, Prologue xi, - xii

27. Neal, Mary C., "To Heaven and Back: A Doctor's Extraordinary Account of Her Death, Heaven, Angels, and Life Again", Colorado Springs, Colorado, WaterBrook Press, 2011, pg 68-69

28. Neal, Mary C., "To Heaven and Back: A Doctor's Extraordinary Account of Her Death, Heaven, Angels, and Life Again", Colorado Springs, Colorado, WaterBrook Press, 2011, pg 70-71

29. Neal, Mary C., "To Heaven and Back: A Doctor's Extraordinary Account of Her Death, Heaven, Angels, and Life Again", Colorado Springs, Colorado, WaterBrook Press, 2011, pg 73-74

30. Guggenheim, Bill and Guggenheim Judy,"Hello From Heaven!", New York, New York, Bantam Books. 1995, pg 133

31. Brinkley, Dannion, "Saved by the Light", New York, New York, HarperCollins Publishers, 2008, pg 5,8

32. Moody, Raymond A. Jr, "Life After Life", New York, NY, Published by Bantam Books in arrangement with Mockingbird Books, 1975, pg 58

33. Brinkley, Dannion, "Saved by the Light", New York, New York, HarperCollins Publishers, 2008, pg 9

34. Morse, Melvin L.,"*Closer To The Light: Learning From the Near-Death Experiences of Children*", New York, New York, Ivy Books, 1990, pg 132,134

35. Brinkley, Dannion, "*Saved by the Light*", New York, New York, HarperCollins Publishers, 2008, pg 10

36. Brinkley, Dannion, "*Saved by the Light*", New York, New York, HarperCollins Publishers, 2008, pg 14-19

37. Brinkley, Dannion, "*Saved by the Light*", New York, New York, HarperCollins Publishers, 2008, pg 19

38. Brinkley, Dannion, "*Saved by the Light*", New York, New York, HarperCollins Publishers, 2008, pg 19

39. Walsch, Neale Donald "*The New Revealations: A Conversation With God*" New York, New York: Atria Books, 2002, pg 126-127

40. Moorjani, Anita, "*Dying To Be Me: My Journey from Cancer, To Near Death, To True Healing*", New York, New York, Hay House Inc.,2012, pg 56,59-60

41. Moorjani, Anita, "*Dying To Be Me: My Journey from Cancer, To Near Death, To True Healing*", New York, New York, Hay House Inc.,2012, pg 60,61

42. Moorjani, Anita, "*Dying To Be Me: My Journey from Cancer, To Near Death, To True Healing*", New York, New York, Hay House Inc.,2012, pg 63

43. Moorjani, Anita, *"Dying To Be Me: My Journey from Cancer, To Near Death, To True Healing"*, New York, New York, Hay House Inc.,2012, pg 66,67,68

44. Moorjani, Anita, *"Dying To Be Me: My Journey from Cancer, To Near Death, To True Healing"*, New York, New York, Hay House Inc.,2012, pg 69

45. Moorjani, Anita, *"Dying To Be Me: My Journey from Cancer, To Near Death, To True Healing"*, New York, New York, Hay House Inc.,2012, pg 70

46. Masaru, Emoto,*"Hidden Messages in Water"*, New York, New York, Atria Books, 2001, pg 8

47. Moorjani, Anita, *"Dying To Be Me: My Journey from Cancer, To Near Death, To True Healing"*, New York, New York, Hay House Inc.,2012, pg 74,75

48. Moorjani, Anita, *"Dying To Be Me: My Journey from Cancer, To Near Death, To True Healing"*, New York, New York, Hay House Inc.,2012, pg 76

49. Moorjani, Anita, *"Dying To Be Me: My Journey from Cancer, To Near Death, To True Healing"*, New York, New York, Hay House Inc.,2012, pg 79-82

50. Alexander, Eben,*"Proof of Heaven: A Neurosurgeon's Journey into the Afterlife"*, New York, New York, Simon & Schuster Inc.,2012, pg 7

51. Alexander, Eben,"Proof of Heaven: A Neurosurgeon's Journey into the Afterlife", New York, New York, Simon & Schuster Inc.,2012, pg 8

52. Alexander, Eben,"Proof of Heaven: A Neurosurgeon's Journey into the Afterlife", New York, New York, Simon & Schuster Inc.,2012, pg 35

53. Alexander, Eben,"Proof of Heaven: A Neurosurgeon's Journey into the Afterlife", New York, New York, Simon & Schuster Inc.,2012, pg 14-16,29-32,38,92

54. Alexander, Eben,"Proof of Heaven: A Neurosurgeon's Journey into the Afterlife", New York, New York, Simon & Schuster Inc.,2012, pg 38

55. Alexander, Eben,"Proof of Heaven: A Neurosurgeon's Journey into the Afterlife", New York, New York, Simon & Schuster Inc.,2012, pg 40-41,47

56. Alexander, Eben,"Proof of Heaven: A Neurosurgeon's Journey into the Afterlife", New York, New York, Simon & Schuster Inc.,2012, pg 47

57. Alexander, Eben,"Proof of Heaven: A Neurosurgeon's Journey into the Afterlife", New York, New York, Simon & Schuster Inc.,2012, pg 46-48,68-69,76-79,105-107,112-120

58. Alexander, Eben,"Proof of Heaven: A Neurosurgeon's Journey into the Afterlife", New York, New York, Simon & Schuster Inc.,2012, pg 73

59. Walsch, Neale Donald, *"Conversations With God: An Uncommon Dialogue book 1"*- Hardcover, New York: G.P. Putman's Sons,1996, pg 4-5.

60. Walsch, Neale. Donald, *"Conversations With God: An Uncommon Dialogue, Book 3."* 1998 Charlottesville, Virginia: Hampton Roads Publishing Company Inc., pg 224

61. Walsch, Neale. Donald, *"Conversations With God: An Uncommon Dialogue, Book 2."* 1997 Charlottesville, Virginia: Hampton Roads Publishing Company Inc., pg 86

62. Schucman, Helen and Thetford, William, A Course in Miracles, Third Edition, Mill Valley, California: Foundation For Inner Peace, 2007, T-14.IV.8:4,5

63. Walsch, Neale Donald *"The New Revealations: A Conversation With God"*, New York, New York: Atria Books, 2002, pg 31-33,304-305.

64. Walsch, Neale Donald *"The New Revealations: A Conversation With God"*, New York, New York: Atria Books, 2002, pg 125

65. Alexander, Eben,"Proof of Heaven: *A Neurosurgeon's Journey into the Afterlife"*, New York, New York, Simon & Schuster Inc.,2012, pg 48

66. Schucman, Helen and Thetford, William, A Course in Miracles, Third Edition, Mill Valley, California: Foundation For Inner Peace, 2007, T-31.I.3:2,3,4

67. Brinkley, Dannion, *"At Peace In the Light"*, New York, New York, HarperCollins Publishers, 1995, pg 38

68. Schucman, Helen and Thetford, William," *A Course in Miracles"*, Third Edition, Mill Valley,California: Foundation For Inner Peace, 2007, T-31.I.3:2,3,4

69. Walsch, Neale. Donald, *"Conversations With God: An Uncommon Dialogue, Book 3."* 1998 Charlottesville, Virginia: Hampton Roads Publishing Company Inc., pg 186

70. Prophet, Elizabeth Clare,*"Reincarnation: The Missing Link in Christianity"*, Gardiner, Montana, Summit University Press, 1997, pg 45

71. Prophet, Elizabeth Clare,*"Reincarnation: The Missing Link in Christianity"*, Gardiner, Montana, Summit University Press, 1997, pg 225

72. Armstrong, Karen,*"A History of God"*, New York, New York: Ballantine Books a division of The Random House Publishing Group, 1993, pg 123

73. Prophet, Elizabeth Clare,*"Reincarnation: The Missing Link in Christianity"*, Gardiner, Montana, Summit University Press, 1997, pg 230-231

74. Prophet, Elizabeth Clare,*"Reincarnation: The Missing Link in Christianity"*, Gardiner, Montana, Summit University Press, 1997, pg 226-227

75. Armstrong, Karen,"*A History of God*", New York, New York: Ballantine Books a division of The Random House Publishing Group, 1993, pg 123

76. Prophet, Elizabeth Clare,"*Reincarnation: The Missing Link in Christianity*", Gardiner, Montana, Summit University Press, 1997, pg 228-230

77. Prophet, Elizabeth Clare,"*Reincarnation: The Missing Link in Christianity*", Gardiner, Montana, Summit University Press, 1997, pg 51-63.

78. Walsch, Neale. Donald, "*Conversations With God: An Uncommon Dialogue, Book 3.*" 1998 Charlottesville, Virginia: Hampton Roads Publishing Company Inc., pg 127-128.

79. Prophet, Elizabeth Clare,"*Reincarnation: The Missing Link in Christianity*", Gardiner, Montana, Summit University Press, 1997, pg 231-232

80. Prophet, Elizabeth Clare,"*Reincarnation: The Missing Link in Christianity*", Gardiner, Montana, Summit University Press, 1997, pg 232-233

81. Armstrong, Karen,"*A History of God*", New York, New York: Ballantine Books a division of The Random House Publishing Group, 1993, pg 124-125

82. Prophet, Elizabeth Clare,"*Reincarnation: The Missing Link in Christianity*", Gardiner, Montana, Summit University Press, 1997, pg 233

83. Schucman, Helen and Thetford, William," *A Course in Miracles*", Third Edition, Mill Valley, California: Foundation For Inner Peace, 2007, T-2.I.1:2,3,4

84. Walsch, Neale. Donald, *"Conversations With God: An Uncommon Dialogue, Book 2."* 1997 Charlottesville, Virginia: Hampton Roads Publishing Company Inc., pg 31

85. Schucman, Helen and Thetford, William," *A Course in Miracles*", Third Edition, Mill Valley, California: Foundation For Inner Peace, 2007, T-1.V.1:4,5,6,7,8

86. Walsch, Neale. Donald, *"Conversations With God: An Uncommon Dialogue, Book 2."* 1997 Charlottesville, Virginia: Hampton Roads Publishing Company Inc., pg 53

87. Walsch, Neale Donald, *"Conversations With God: An Uncommon Dialogue book 1"*- Hardcover, New York: G.P. Putman's Sons,1996, pg 28

88. Walsch, Neale. Donald, *"Conversations With God: An Uncommon Dialogue, Book 3."* 1998 Charlottesville, Virginia: Hampton Roads Publishing Company Inc., pg 178-179

89. Schucman, Helen and Thetford, William," *A Course in Miracles*", Third Edition, Mill Valley, California: Foundation For Inner Peace, 2007, W-PII.223.1:1,2

90. Walsch, Neale. Donald, *"Conversations With God: An Uncommon Dialogue, Book 3."* 1998 Charlottesville, Virginia: Hampton Roads Publishing Company Inc., pg 61

91. Mills, Roy,"*A Soul's Remembrance: Earth is Not Our Home*", Bellevue, Washington: Onjinjinkta Publishing, 1999, pg 29-30

92. Walsch, Neale. Donald, "*Conversations With God: An Uncommon Dialogue, Book 3.*" 1998 Charlottesville, Virginia: Hampton Roads Publishing Company Inc., pg 98

93. Alexander, Eben,"Proof of Heaven: *A Neurosurgeon's Journey into the Afterlife*", New York, New York, Simon & Schuster Inc.,2012, pg 48

94. Walsch, Neale Donald, "*Conversations With God: An Uncommon Dialogue book 1*"- Hardcover, New York: G.P. Putman's Sons,1996, pg 29

95. Walsch, Neale Donald, "*Conversations With God: An Uncommon Dialogue book 1*"- Hardcover, New York: G.P. Putman's Sons,1996, pg 24

96. Howe, Caroline, "Exclusive: How Gambino mobster went from a Goodfella to a Dogfella when he rescued a sickly 7-pound Shih Tzu with maggots and a broken jaw tied to a parking meter", www. Dailymail.co.uk,2015, news/article/3101532

97. Walsch, Neale Donald "*The New Revealations: A Conversation With God*", New York, New York: Atria Books, 2002, pg 59-60

98. Schucman, Helen and Thetford, William," *A Course in Miracles*", Third Edition, Mill Valley, California: Foundation For Inner Peace, 2007, T-2.III.3.1:3-6

99. Schucman, Helen and Thetford, William," *A Course in Miracles*", Third Edition, Mill Valley, California: Foundation For Inner Peace, 2007, T-31.VII.3:1-2

100. Walsch, Neale. Donald, "*Conversations With God: An Uncommon Dialogue, Book 2.*" 1997 Charlottesville, Virginia: Hampton Roads Publishing Company Inc., pg 191-192

101. Walsch, Neale. Donald, "*Conversations With God: An Uncommon Dialogue, Book 3.*" 1998 Charlottesville, Virginia: Hampton Roads Publishing Company Inc., pg 127

102. Walsch, Neale. Donald, "*Conversations With God: An Uncommon Dialogue, Book 3.*" 1998 Charlottesville, Virginia: Hampton Roads Publishing Company Inc., pg 86-87

103. Walsch, Neale Donald "*The New Revealations: A Conversation With God*", New York, New York: Atria Books, 2002, pg 215-216

104. Strobel, Lee, "*A Case for a Creator, A Journalist Investigates Scientific Evidence that Points to God*", Grand Rapids, Michigan, Zondervan, pg 160-161

105. Radin, Dean, "*The Conscious Universe, The Scientific Truth of Psychic Phenomena*", New York, New York, HarperCollins Publishers, 2009, pg 153-155

106. Radin, Dean, "*The Conscious Universe, The Scientific Truth of Psychic Phenomena*", New York, New York, HarperCollins Publishers, 2009, Book back cover, pg viii, xiv

107. Radin, Dean, *"The Conscious Universe, The Scientific Truth of Psychic Phenomena"*, New York, New York, HarperCollins Publishers, 2009, pg xiv

108. McTaggart, Lynne, *"The Field: The Quest for the Secret Force of the Universe"*, New York, New York: HarperCollins Publishers, 2002, pg 106-108,113

109. McTaggart, Lynne, *"The Field: The Quest for the Secret Force of the Universe"*, New York, New York: HarperCollins Publishers, 2002, pg 116-118

110. Radin, Dean, *"The Conscious Universe, The Scientific Truth of Psychic Phenomena"*, New York, New York, HarperCollins Publishers, 2009, pg 73,103-104

111. Radin, Dean, *"The Conscious Universe, The Scientific Truth of Psychic Phenomena"*, New York, New York, HarperCollins Publishers, 2009, pg 213

112. McTaggart, Lynne, *"The Field: The Quest for the Secret Force of the Universe"*, New York, New York: HarperCollins Publishers, 2002, pg 149-155

113. Radin, Dean, *"The Conscious Universe, The Scientific Truth of Psychic Phenomena"*, New York, New York, HarperCollins Publishers, 2009, pg 214-215

114. Radin, Dean, *"The Conscious Universe, The Scientific Truth of Psychic Phenomena"*, New York, New York, HarperCollins Publishers, 2009, pg 215-216

115.   Radin, Dean, *"The Conscious Universe, The Scientific Truth of Psychic Phenomena"*, New York, New York, HarperCollins Publishers, 2009, pg 21

116.   McTaggart, Lynne, *"The Field: The Quest for the Secret Force of the Universe"*, New York, New York: HarperCollins Publishers, 2002, pg 181-182

117.   McTaggart, Lynne, *"The Field: The Quest for the Secret Force of the Universe"*, New York, New York: HarperCollins Publishers, 2002, pg 188-190

118.   McTaggart, Lynne, *"The Field: The Quest for the Secret Force of the Universe"*, New York, New York: HarperCollins Publishers, 2002, pg 181,191,193

119.   Walsch, Neale. Donald, *"Conversations With God: An Uncommon Dialogue, Book 3."* 1998 Charlottesville, Virginia: Hampton Roads Publishing Company Inc., pg 59

120.   Radin, Dean, *"The Conscious Universe, The Scientific Truth of Psychic Phenomena"*, New York, New York, HarperCollins Publishers, 2009, pg 126

121.   Radin, Dean, *"The Conscious Universe, The Scientific Truth of Psychic Phenomena"*, New York, New York, HarperCollins Publishers, 2009, pg 125-130

122.   Talbot, Michael, *"The Holographic Universe: The Revolutionary Theory of Reality"*, New York, New York: HarperCollins Publishers, 1991, pg 210

123. Radin, Dean, *"The Conscious Universe, The Scientific Truth of Psychic Phenomena"*, New York, New York, HarperCollins Publishers, 2009, pg xx

124. Walsch, Neale. Donald, *"Conversations With God: An Uncommon Dialogue, Book 3."* 1998 Charlottesville, Virginia: Hampton Roads Publishing Company Inc., pg 113

125. Radin, Dean, *"The Conscious Universe, The Scientific Truth of Psychic Phenomena"*, New York, New York, HarperCollins Publishers, 2009, pg 306

126. Talbot, Michael, *"The Holographic Universe: The Revolutionary Theory of Reality"*, New York, New York: HarperCollins Publishers, 1991, pg 121

127. Talbot, Michael, *"The Holographic Universe: The Revolutionary Theory of Reality"*, New York, New York: HarperCollins Publishers, 1991, pg 91

128. Talbot, Michael, *"The Holographic Universe: The Revolutionary Theory of Reality"*, New York, New York: HarperCollins Publishers, 1991, pg 96

129. Talbot, Michael, *"The Holographic Universe: The Revolutionary Theory of Reality"*, New York, New York: HarperCollins Publishers, 1991, pg 97-100

130. Talbot, Michael, *"The Holographic Universe: The Revolutionary Theory of Reality"*, New York, New York: HarperCollins Publishers, 1991, pg 100-101

131. Moorjani, Anita, *"Dying To Be Me: My Journey from Cancer, To Near Death, To True Healing"*, New York, New York, Hay House Inc.,2012, pg 75

132. Talbot, Michael, *"The Holographic Universe: The Revolutionary Theory of Reality"*, New York, New York: HarperCollins Publishers, 1991, pg 117-118

133. Schucman, Helen and Thetford, William," *A Course in Miracles"*, Third Edition, Mill Valley, California: Foundation For Inner Peace, 2007, T-2.VI.9.1:3-6

134. Talbot, Michael, *"The Holographic Universe: The Revolutionary Theory of Reality"*, New York, New York: HarperCollins Publishers, 1991, pg 83-87

135. Talbot, Michael, *"The Holographic Universe: The Revolutionary Theory of Reality"*, New York, New York: HarperCollins Publishers, 1991, pg 112

136. Brinkley, Dannion, *"At Peace in the Light"*, New York, New York, HarperCollins Publishers, 1996, pg 104

137. Talbot, Michael, *"The Holographic Universe: The Revolutionary Theory of Reality"*, New York, New York: HarperCollins Publishers, 1991, pg 174-178

138. Walsch, Neale. Donald, *"Conversations With God: An Uncommon Dialogue, Book 3."* 1998 Charlottesville, Virginia: Hampton Roads Publishing Company Inc., pg 170

139. Schwartz, Gary E., " *The Afterlife Experiments: Breakthrough Scientific Evidence of the Life After Death*", New York, New York, Atria Books, 2002, Back book cover, pg 178-179, 260

140. Schwartz, Gary E., " The Afterlife Experiments: Breakthrough Scientific Evidence of the Life After Death", New York, New York, Atria Books, 2002, pg 216-217

141. Lanza, Robert, "*Biocentrism: How Life and Consciousness are the Keys to Understanding the True Nature of the Universe*", Dallas, Texas, BenBella Books Inc.,2010, pg 91-92

142. Strobel, Lee "A Case for a Creator: "A Journalist Investigates Scientific Evidence that Points to God", Grand Rapids, Michigan, Zondervan, 2004, pg 36,42

143. Strobel, Lee "A Case for a Creator: "A Journalist Investigates Scientific Evidence that Points to God", Grand Rapids, Michigan, Zondervan, 2004, pg 43-45

144. Strobel, Lee "A Case for a Creator: "A Journalist Investigates Scientific Evidence that Points to God", Grand Rapids, Michigan, Zondervan, 2004, pg 32

145. Strobel, Lee "A Case for a Creator: "A Journalist Investigates Scientific Evidence that Points to God", Grand Rapids, Michigan, Zondervan, 2004, pg 125-152

146. Strobel, Lee "A Case for a Creator: "A Journalist Investigates Scientific Evidence that Points to God", Grand Rapids, Michigan, Zondervan, 2004, pg 78,126,130-131

147. Strobel, Lee "A Case for a Creator: "A Journalist Investigates Scientific Evidence that Points to God", Grand Rapids, Michigan, Zondervan, 2004, pg 136

148. Walsch, Neale. Donald, *"Conversations With God: An Uncommon Dialogue, Book 3."* 1998 Charlottesville, Virginia: Hampton Roads Publishing Company Inc., pg 324

149. Talbot, Michael, *"The Holographic Universe: The Revolutionary Theory of Reality"*, New York, New York: HarperCollins Publishers, 1991, pg 33-34

150. Lanza, Robert, *"Biocentrism: How Life and Consciousness are the Keys to Understanding the True Nature of the Universe"*, Dallas, Texas, BenBella Books Inc.,2010, pg 50-52

151. Lanza, Robert, *"Biocentrism: How Life and Consciousness are the Keys to Understanding the True Nature of the Universe"*, Dallas, Texas, BenBella Books Inc.,2010, pg 50-52, 80-81

152. McTaggart, Lynne, *"The Field: The Quest for the Secret Force of the Universe"*, New York, New York: HarperCollins Publishers, 2002, pg 36,96,144

153. Walsch, Neale. Donald, *"Conversations With God: An Uncommon Dialogue, Book 2."* 1997 Charlottesville, Virginia: Hampton Roads Publishing Company Inc., pg 87

154. Masaru, Emoto,*"Hidden Messages in Water"*, New York, New York, Atria Books, 2001, Prologue xx - xxviii

155. Lanza, Robert, *"Biocentrism: How Life and Consciousness are the Keys to Understanding the True Nature of the Universe"*, Dallas, Texas, BenBella Books Inc.,2010, pg 2

156. Walsch, Neale. Donald, *"Conversations With God: An Uncommon Dialogue, Book 2."* 1997 Charlottesville, Virginia: Hampton Roads Publishing Company Inc., pg 158

157. Mills, Roy,*"A Soul's Remembrance: Earth is Not Our Home"*, Bellevue, Washington: Onjinjinkta Publishing, 1999, pg 105

158. Schucman, Helen and Thetford, William," *A Course in Miracles"*, Third Edition, Mill Valley, California: Foundation For Inner Peace, 2007, T-13.XI.3:8-13

159. Walsch, Neale Donald, *"Conversations With God: An Uncommon Dialogue book 1"*- Hardcover, New York, New York, G.P. Putman's Sons,1996, pg 194

160. Schwartz, Robert (2007). *"Your Soul's Plan: Discovering the Real Meaning of the Life You Planned. Berkeley"*, California, USA, Frog Books, 2007, pg 15,29,30,81

161. Walsch, Neale. Donald, *"Conversations With God: An Uncommon Dialogue, Book 2."* 1997 Charlottesville, Virginia: Hampton Roads Publishing Company Inc., pg 50

162. Schwartz, Robert (2007). *"Your Soul's Plan: Discovering the Real Meaning of the Life You Planned. Berkeley"*, California, USA, Frog Books, 2007, pg 68,77,79

163. Walsch, Neale Donald, *"Conversations With God: An Uncommon Dialogue book 1"*- Hardcover, New York, New York, G.P. Putman's Sons,1996, pg 45,46

164. Schwartz, Robert (2007). *"Your Soul's Plan: Discovering the Real Meaning of the Life You Planned.* Berkeley", California, USA, Frog Books, 2007, pg 21-22,119,160-161

165. Schwartz, Robert (2007). *"Your Soul's Plan: Discovering the Real Meaning of the Life You Planned.* Berkeley", California, USA, Frog Books, 2007, pg 52-53,57-58,66,70,170,247,254-255,259

166. Schwartz, Robert (2007). *"Your Soul's Plan: Discovering the Real Meaning of the Life You Planned.* Berkeley", California, USA, Frog Books, 2007, pg 200-201

167. Walsch, Neale Donald, *"Conversations With God: An Uncommon Dialogue book 1"*- Hardcover, New York, New York, G.P. Putman's Sons,1996, pg 49

168. Sittser, Gerald L.,*"A Grace Disquised: How the Soul Grows Through Loss"*, Grand Rapids, Michigan, Zondervan, Hardcover, 1995, inside back cover.

169. Sittser, Gerald L.,*"A Grace Disquised: How the Soul Grows Through Loss"*, Grand Rapids, Michigan, Zondervan, Hardcover,1995, pg 25-26

170. Sittser, Gerald L.,*"A Grace Disquised: How the Soul Grows Through Loss"*, Grand Rapids, Michigan, Zondervan, Hardcover,1995, pg 134-135

171. Sittser, Gerald L.,"*A Grace Disquised: How the Soul Grows Through Loss*", Grand Rapids, Michigan, Zondervan, Hardcover,1995, pg 137

172. Schucman, Helen and Thetford, William," *A Course in Miracles*", Third Edition, Mill Valley, California: Foundation For Inner Peace, 2007, W-P1.62.3:1

173. Sittser, Gerald L.,"*A Grace Disquised: How the Soul Grows Through Loss*", Grand Rapids, Michigan, Zondervan, Hardcover,1995, pg 137

174. Mills, Roy,"*A Soul's Remembrance: Earth is Not Our Home*", Bellevue, Washington: Onjinjinkta Publishing, 1999, pg 121,122

175. Schwartz, Robert (2007). "*Your Soul's Plan: Discovering the Real Meaning of the Life You Planned. Berkeley*", California, USA, Frog Books, 2007, pg 67,81

176. Schwartz, Robert (2007). "*Your Soul's Plan: Discovering the Real Meaning of the Life You Planned. Berkeley*", California, USA, Frog Books, 2007, pg 67,81

177. Walsch, Neale. Donald, "*Conversations With God: An Uncommon Dialogue, Book 2.*" 1997 Charlottesville, Virginia: Hampton Roads Publishing Company Inc., pg 156

178. Schwartz, Robert (2007). "*Your Soul's Plan: Discovering the Real Meaning of the Life You Planned. Berkeley*", California, USA, Frog Books, 2007, pg 48-49,55

179. Mills, Roy,"*A Soul's Remembrance: Earth is Not Our Home*", Bellevue, Washington: Onjinjinkta Publishing, 1999, pg 117

180. Abrams, Michael, "*The Evolutionary Angel: An Emergency Physician's Lessons with Death and the Divine*", Boulder, Colorado, Abundance Media 2000,(1999), pg 68-69

181. Mills, Roy,"*A Soul's Remembrance: Earth is Not Our Home*", Bellevue, Washington: Onjinjinkta Publishing, 1999, pg 119-120

182. Walsch, Neale. Donald, "*Conversations With God: An Uncommon Dialogue, Book 2.*" 1997 Charlottesville, Virginia: Hampton Roads Publishing Company Inc., pg 156

183. Mills, Roy,"*A Soul's Remembrance: Earth is Not Our Home*", Bellevue, Washington: Onjinjinkta Publishing, 1999, pg 117

184. Schwartz, Robert (2007). "*Your Soul's Plan: Discovering the Real Meaning of the Life You Planned*. Berkeley*", California, USA, Frog Books, 2007, pg 20

185. Walsch, Neale Donald, "*Conversations With God: An Uncommon Dialogue book 1*"- Hardcover, New York, New York, G.P. Putman's Sons,1996, pg 46

186. Schwartz, Robert (2007). "*Your Soul's Plan: Discovering the Real Meaning of the Life You Planned*. Berkeley*", California, USA, Frog Books, 2007, pg 68,79

187. Breast Cancer Research Foundation: www./bcrfcure.org/ history

188. Schwartz, Robert (2007). *"Your Soul's Plan: Discovering the Real Meaning of the Life You Planned.* Berkeley", California, USA, Frog Books, 2007, pg 80

189. Schwartz, Robert (2007). *"Your Soul's Plan: Discovering the Real Meaning of the Life You Planned.* Berkeley", California, USA, Frog Books, 2007, pg 57

190. Schucman, Helen and Thetford, William," *A Course in Miracles*", Third Edition, Mill Valley, California: Foundation For Inner Peace, 2007, W-P1.47.7:3-6

191. Schucman, Helen and Thetford, William," *A Course in Miracles*", Third Edition, Mill Valley, California: Foundation For Inner Peace, 2007, T-8.VII.5:3-4

192. Walsch, Neale. Donald, *"Conversations With God: An Uncommon Dialogue, Book 3."* 1998 Charlottesville, Virginia: Hampton Roads Publishing Company Inc., pg 143

193. Schucman, Helen and Thetford, William," *A Course in Miracles*", Third Edition, Mill Valley, California: Foundation For Inner Peace, 2007, T-9.VIII.10:8-9

194. Schucman, Helen and Thetford, William," *A Course in Miracles*", Third Edition, Mill Valley, California: Foundation For Inner Peace, 2007, T-9.VIII.7:1-6

195. Walsch, Neale. Donald, *"Conversations With God: An Uncommon Dialogue, Book 3."* 1998 Charlottesville, Virginia: Hampton Roads Publishing Company Inc., pg 65-66

BIBLIOGRAPHY

Abrams, M. (1999). *The Evolution Angel, An Emergency Physician's Lessions with Death and the Divine.* Boulder, Colorado: Abundance Media 2000.

Alexander, E. (2012). *Proof of Heaven: A Neurosurgeon's Journey into the Afterlife.* New York, New York: Simon & Schuster Paperbacks.

Armstrong, K. (1993). *A History of God.* New York, New York: Ballantine Books a division of The Random House Publishing Group.

Brinkley, D. (1995). *At Peace in the Light.* New York, New York: HarperCollins Publishers.

Brinkley, D. (2008). *Saved by the Light.* New York, New York: HarperCollins Publishers.

Eadie, B. J. (1992). *Embraced by the Light.* Placerville, California: Green Leaf Press.

Emoto, M. (2004). *The Hidden Messages in Water:.* Hillsboro, Oregon, USA: Beyond Words Publishing Inc.

Gerry, S. (1995). *A Grace Disguised: How the Soul Grows Through Loss.* Grand Rapids, Michigan, USA: Zondervan.

Guggenheim, J., & Guggenheim, B. (1995). *Hello From Heaven.* New York, New York: Bantam Books.

Howe, C. (2015). *How Gambino mobster went from a Goodfella to a Dogfella when he rescued a sickly seven-pound Shih Tzu with maggots and a broken jaw tied to a parking meter.* World Wide Web: Daily Mail.com.

Lanza, R., & Berman, B. (2009). *Biocentrism, How Life and Consciousness are the Keys to Understanding the True Nature of the Universe.* Dallas, Texas: BenBella Books Inc.

Long, J., & Perry, P. (2010). *Evidence of the Afterlife.* New York, New York: HarperCollins Publishers.

McTaggart, L. (2002). *The Field: The Quest for the Secret Force of the Universe.* New York, New York: HarperCollins Publishers.

Mills, R. (1999). *A Soul's Remembrance: Earth is Not Our Home.* Bellevue, Washington: Onjinjinkta Publishing.

Moorjani, A. (2012). *Dying to be Me: My Journey from Cancer, To Near-Death, To Healing.* New York, New York: Hay House Inc.

Morse, M. (1990). *Closer to the Light, Learning from the Near-Death Experience of Children.* New York, New York: Random House Publishing Group.

Neal, M. (2012). *To Heaven and Back.* Colorado Springs, Colorado: Waterbrook Press.

Parnia, S. (2006). *What Happens When We Die.* New York, New York: Hay House Inc.

Perry, D. B. (1996). *At Peace in the Light*. Unknown: HarperCollins Pubhishing.

Prophet, E. C. (1997). *Reincarnation - The Missing Link in Christianity*. Gardiner, Montana, USA: Summit University Press.

Radin, D. (1997). *The Conscious Universe: The Scientific Truth of Psychic Phenomena*. Unknown: HarperCollins Publishers.

Ring, K., & Cooper, S. (1999). *Mindsight*. Palo Alto, California: William James Center of Consiousness Studies at the Institute of Transpersonal Psychology.

Schucman, H., & Thetford, W. (2007). *A Course In Miracles, Third Edition*. Mill Valley, California: Foundation For Inner Peace.

Schwartz, G., & Simon, W. (2002). *The Afterlife Experiments: Breakthrough Scientific Evidence of Life After Death*. New York, New York: Atria Books.

Schwartz, R. (2007). *Your Soul's Plan: Discovering the Real Meaning of the Life You Planned*. Berkeley, California, USA: Frog Books, an imprint of North Atlantic Books.

Sittser, G. L. (1995). *A Grace Disguised*. Grand Rapids, Michigan: Zondervan.

Strobel, L. (2004). *A Case for a Creator, A Journalist Investigates Scientific Evidence that Points to God*. Grand Rapids, Michigan: Zondervan.

Talbot, M. (1991). *The Holographic Universe: The Revolutionary Theory of Reality.* New York, New York: HarperCollins Publishers.

Walsch, N. D. (1996). *Conversations With God: An Uncommon Dialogue book 1.* New York: G.P. Putman's Sons.

Walsch, N. D. (1997). *Conversations With God: An Uncommon Dialogue Book 2.* Charlottesville, Virginia: Hampton Roads Publishing Company Inc.

Walsch, N. D. (1998). *Conversations With God: An Uncommon Dialogue, Book 3.* Charlottesville, Virginia: Hampton Roads Publishing Company Inc.

Walsch, N. D. (2002). *The New Revealations: A Conversation With God.* New York, New York: Atria Books.

INDEX

35226953R00127

Made in the USA
Middletown, DE
24 September 2016